THE
GOD
FACTOR

Getting the Edge at Work

THE
GOD
FACTOR

Getting the Edge at Work

DR. MARCUS D. HESTER

Treasure House

An Imprint of

Destiny Image® Publishers, Inc.

P.O. Box 310

Shippensburg, PA 17257-0310

"For where your treasure is, there will your heart be also."
Matthew 6:21

ISBN 0-7684-2953-6

For Worldwide Distribution
Printed in the U.S.A.

This book and all other Destiny Image, Revival Press, MercyPlace, Fresh Bread, Destiny Image Fiction, and Treasure House books are available at Christian bookstores and distributors worldwide.

2 3 4 5 6 7 8 9 10 / 09 08 07 06 05 04

For a U.S. bookstore nearest you, call 1-800-722-6774.
For more information on foreign distributors, call 717-532-3040.
Or reach us on the Internet:

www.destinyimage.com

ENDORSEMENTS

How refreshing to read a book that speaks with clarity to a significant change in the Body of Christ! God is tearing down walls that have formed divisions between those in "spiritual" places of employment and those in "secular" jobs. Marcus Hester does an outstanding job of removing religious glasses and presenting a prophetic picture of where the Lord is taking the Church. I highly recommend *The God Factor* to all who have a desire to hear what the Spirit is saying to the Church today.

—Barbara Wentroble
Author; Founding Apostle, IBM Apostolic Network

One of the strongest and loudest things the Spirit is saying to the churches these days is, "Release My marketplace ministers for the destiny I have given them!" Marcus Hester has not only heard this word, but his timely book, *The God Factor*, opens new windows and sheds strategic light on what all of this means for you and me. This is a book you will not want to miss!

—C. Peter Wagner
Presiding Apostle, International Coalition of Apostles (ICA)

At every intersection on a new highway there must be clear signposts to guide the way. Marcus Hester has set up some very clear signs for the reader to follow as we move into a new era and a new revelation of God's plan. He is well qualified to do this, since he has already been down the road and knows the way. This book is essential for those who are not content with the status quo and are ready to move on to the fresh things God is doing in this hour. The many thought-provoking "one-liners" will force you to stop and think about the present course you are taking. They will no doubt push you into a whole new understanding and new agenda.

—Don Lyon
Senior Pastor, Faith Center
Rockford, IL

Marcus Hester takes all past teaching on the subject of the marketplace movement to a new level of completeness. This book integrates the marketplace movement with the apostolic movement. It goes beyond the basics of the movement to knowledge, revelation and prophetic fulfillment on this fresh move of God. It is a must-read for all Christians!

—Apostle John P. Kelly
Director, Leadership Education for Apostolic Development

Marcus's transparency on the subject of interpreting and answering his call to ministry in the workplace was born out of his personal struggle of being raised in a ministry family in the traditional church model. Feeling called to serve the Kingdom with great passion but without a specific place where he "fit," he discovered marketplace ministry. This is a true prophetic word for this season.

—Kevin Leal
Key Ministries

The nagging question regarding the development of the extended church in the marketplace is: How are the traditional church and the extended church going to function together? At last someone has addressed the issues that are sure to arise between the leaders of both churches. Marcus Hester has addressed this relationship in a straightforward manner that will provide a blueprint for how the Church and the marketplace go forward.

—Linda Rios Brook
President, Lakeland Leadership League
Dean of LifeWorks, a division of the Wagner Leadership Institute

Marcus Hester has captured what the Spirit is saying to the Christian leaders in these last days before Christ comes for His Bride. This book sheds fresh new light on our destiny to join God where He is at work.

—Marjorie Hester, mother
Vice President, Missionary Encourages, Inc.

It is exciting to watch God birth a new movement that is designed to equip and release believers in the workplace to bring transformation. With new movements come new voices and new revelations about what God is doing and the changes that will be coming. Marcus has given us a glimpse of things to come in the faith and work movement. *The God Factor* is a must-read for anyone who wants to look into the future of workplace ministry, especially as it relates to the local church.

—Os Hillman
Director, International Coalition of Workplace Ministries

The God Factor is a manifesto for spiritual revolution in the marketplace. Christian men and women in the marketplace are crying out to God, asking Him how they can be more effective in their daily lives. *The God Factor* will answer those questions, and affirm them in their unique calling to transform the marketplace with the good news of Jesus Christ.

—Paul Gazelka, Businessman
Author, *Marketplace Ministers*

Marcus Hester has a unique insight and burden concerning marketplace ministry. I have known him for many years and have seen his increased knowledge and revelation in this area. He is a pioneer in developing marketplace ministers in the Church. His latest book, *The God Factor*, is a must-read for any believers desiring to keep current in what God is doing in the marketplace. I highly recommend it and look forward to the lasting fruit it will bring.

—Apostle John Eckhardt
Crusaders Ministries Founder and CEO of Impact Ministries

Dr. Hester has compiled a comprehensive presentation of the apostolic move in the marketplace. The biblical foundation he has established, together with his practical insights gained through research and experience, offer clarity and momentum to God's move.

—Dr. "Buddy" Crum
Pastor, Life Center Ministries
CEO, International Christian Marketplace Alliance

One of God's decisions is for revival to reach people of all walks of life, most importantly the workplace. Marcus Hester's timely book, *The God Factor*, is an incredible tool in God's hands. Get one in yours! It will help you reach your marketplace powerfully and effectively. This is a must-read for all!

—Apostle Mary Alice Isleib
Mary Alice Isleib Ministries

In every generation God, by His sovereign purposes and His powerful plans, raises some Issachars. An Issachar is someone who has tapped into the heart and mind of God, who understands the times and knows what to do.

In this third day of God, one of the modern-day Issachars is Apostle Marcus Hester. His new book, *The God Factor*, is full of *rhema* and revelation of what God is doing in this season.

Apostle Hester has tapped into the next great move of God: the empowerment of God's people to do Kingdom work outside the walls of the church in the area where we spend most of our lives…the marketplace.

I highly recommend this book to anyone and to everyone who has a desire to tap into the plan, purposes and power of God in this new millennium.

—Apostle H. Daniel Wilson
Senior Pastor, Valley Kingdom Min. Intl.

Contents

FOREWORD

I once heard a consultant talk about the "Principle of the Slight Edge." He said, "Those who succeed in business are those who work slightly harder, who spend just a little more time than anyone else." He called that the "Principle of the Slight Edge." Thank you, Marcus Hester, you have introduced us all to the "Principle of the Great Edge." It is the God Factor: Those who succeed in business are those who trust God more and spend more time in worship and intimacy with the Father.

Businesspeople around the world are looking for the competitive edge; that one idea that can move them ahead, that one perfectly timed launch, the right connection, or even just plain luck. And occasionally it appears as if one of them has found the right formula. However, most of these searchers are looking in all the wrong places.

The truth is that God wants to give you that competitive edge. He is speaking today more clearly than most of us have ever experienced. Businessmen and women are listening for and hearing the voice of God. They are finding that He is not only interested in their work, but He also wants to bless it; to prosper it; and to become the factor that makes the difference. In my own experience I have seen the word of the Lord come at the right moment to save businesses. I have watched as God snatched a company from the brink of disaster with a clear word and direction for the future. I have seen the frustrated become the anointed, and I have seen the discouraged become the successful CEO. If you want to get the edge at work, this current release from the mind of Marcus Hester is just what you need.

There are books that will help you to become a good Christian business-person. There are also books on the basic principles of business and creative strategies to enable you to succeed. Others have been released in recent years about the coming revival or transforming move of God in the marketplace. But this book is different.

Written by a successful business owner, who is also a trained and gifted apostolic pastor, *The God Factor* makes plain the desire of Father God's heart. He lays out principles that help you; he encourages and challenges; but he also speaks with a prophetic voice about the future of business and the Kingdom. His keen insight allows us to look into the future of the Church and see some of what is on the Father's heart.

God's Kingdom is advancing as never before. I pray that you will be a part of the great army that the Lord is raising up; *the army with the edge!*

—Rich Marshall
Author, God@Work

INTRODUCTION

In the competitive business world, businessmen and women are always trying to get the "edge" in the marketplace. In an effort to improve efficiency and profitability they constantly review processes, evaluate personnel, and rigorously examine the "bottom line." Trying to improve themselves and stay one step ahead of their competitors, these marketplace leaders have read the latest self-help books available, studied the latest innovations in their field, and attended the best seminars available. They consistently endeavor to get the most "bang for their bucks" in their advertising strategies. However, there is one factor that many marketplace leaders have overlooked. They have overlooked *The God Factor!* In an attempt to stay ahead of the pack many in the business world have disregarded the most powerful force in the universe. It is a spiritual energy that will help them in confronting and finding the solutions to their most pressing and challenging problems. It will guide them in avoiding the most common pitfalls in business. It will facilitate the discovery of wisdom, helping them to navigate through the storms encountered in the marketplace.

In this book, you will discover how you can get the edge by implementing the God Factor at work. Not only will you discover how you can get the edge at work with the God Factor, but also you will rediscover the true purpose of work, a vision that has been lost by many.

Many workers cannot wait until Friday comes along (getting a break from work). They are floundering in a maze of meaningless tasks and have lost the joy of their work. They live for the weekends. *The God Factor* will help you rediscover the true purpose of work. You will find yourself looking forward to Monday instead of Friday. I am sure that you have never imagined this possibility. TGIF (Thank God It's Friday) will take on a whole new meaning in your life.

And lastly, you will not only uncover how you can get the edge at work and recover the true meaning of your life's work, but you will also discover that the phenomenon of "God in the workplace" has become an international reality in the Body of Christ. It has become so big that many spiritual and marketplace leaders have concluded that we are in a new move of God called the "Marketplace Movement." Let me give you a few facts on this new movement in the workplace.

The Movement

"5 years ago—only one conference on spirituality and workplace; now there are hundreds."—Business Week *magazine*

"10,000 Bible and prayer groups in the workplaces meet regularly."—Business Week *magazine*

"Today, a spiritual revival is sweeping across Corporate America as people of all stripes are mixing mysticism into their management, importing into office corridors the lessons usually dolled out in churches, temples, mosques. Gone is the old taboo against talking about God at work."—Business Week *magazine*

"…a mostly unorganized mass of believers—a counterculture bubbling up all over corporate America—who want to bridge the traditional divide between spirituality and work. Historically, such folk operate below the radar, on their own or in small workplace groups where they pray or study the Bible. But now they are getting organized and going public to agitate for change." Fortune *magazine, July 16, 2001*

"Ten years ago we could identify only 25 national or international workplace ministries; today we can identify more than 900." Mike McLoughlin, YWAM Marketplace Mission

Biblical Precedent

New Testament—Of Jesus' 132 public appearances, 122 were in the marketplace.

Of 52 parables Jesus told, 45 had a workplace context. Of 40 divine interventions recorded in Acts, 39 were in the marketplace.

Jesus spent more than 50 percent of His adult life as a carpenter until age 30 before He went into a preaching ministry in the workplace. Jesus called 12 workplace individuals, not clergy, to build His Church.

Work is worship—The Hebrew word Avodah *is the root for the word from which we get the words* work *and* worship.

Work in its different forms is mentioned more than 800 times in the Bible, more than all the words used to express worship, music, praise, *and* singing *combined.*

Quotables

"I believe one of the next great moves of God is going to be through the believers in the workplace."—Dr. Billy Graham

"God has begun an evangelism movement in the workplace that has the potential to transform our society as we know it."—Franklin Graham

"I've never seen the activity of God this deeply in the business community as I do right now."—Henry Blackaby

"Workplace ministry will be one of the core future innovations in church ministry."—George Barna, Boiling Point (Regal Publishing)

"Our surveys reveal that 90-97% of Christians have never heard a sermon relating biblical principles to their work life."—Doug Sherman, author, Your Work Matters to God

"Societal transformation is high on God's agenda and the chief catalytic force to bring it about will be Christians ministering in the marketplace."— C. Peter Wagner, Chancellor, Wagner Leadership Institute

"The church in the workplace is the purest form of the Body of Christ today due to its diversity. Workplace believers are less prone to denominational differences because they have a common goal of representing Christ in their workplaces. The movement will break down denominational barriers that have been held in the past."—Os Hillman, International Coalition of Workplace Ministries

"The most common self-inflicted put-down is 'I am not a pastor—I am just a layperson.' This is all part of a clever satanic scheme to neutralize apostles, prophets, evangelists, pastors, and teachers along with the entire army of disciples, already positioned in the marketplace."—Ed Silvoso, Harvest Evangelism, Anointed for Business.

"Indeed, as with first-century Christianity, it all begins in the marketplace, where the disciples of Jesus daily rub shoulders along with the lost."—Foreword written by Bill McCartney, Promise Keepers, in the book Anointed for Business *(Regal Publishing)*

"Someone recently said that the 'First' Reformation took the Word of God to the common man and woman; and the 'Second' Reformation is taking the work of God to the common man and woman. That time is now! The greatest potential ministry in the world today is the marketplace. Christ's greatest labor force is those men and women already in that environment."—Tom Phillips, VP of Training, Billy Graham Evangelistic Association

Media Coverage

July 2001 Fortune *magazine—"God and Business" cover story*

November 1999 Business Week *magazine—"Spirituality in the Workplace"*

Jan/Feb 2003 New Man *magazine—"Faith and Work Movement"*

January and March 2003 issues Business Reform *magazine—"God in the Workplace"*

As you can see from just a few of the available articles, books, and quotations, God is up to something *"big"* in the marketplace! As you read on, I pray you enjoy this book, but better yet…I pray that God will change your life forever in the way you perceive your work…*as you get the edge with the God Factor*!

Section One

God's Transitioning Church

...Calling to the Marketplace

Chapter 1

THE PURSUIT OF TRUE REVIVAL

And afterward, I will pour out My Spirit on all people. Your sons and daughters will prophesy, your old men will dream dreams, your young men will see visions. Even on My servants, both men and women, I will pour out My Spirit in those days. I will show wonders in the heavens and on the earth, blood and fire and billows of smoke (Joel 2:28-30 NIV).

Several years ago I had a life-changing experience. Like most pastors, I wanted our church to grow and reach our community. I wanted it to be relevant for life in the 21st century. After several years of being a "good" pastor, a disturbing restlessness crept into my heart. I was increasingly troubled about our church, our effectiveness in our city, and my relationship with God. I was simply not satisfied. I wanted more! I had good health, a nice home, and a beautiful family. It was clear that God had put this discontentment in my life. Now, I know that the Bible teaches us that we are to be "content" in all situations as we have much (plenty) or as we have little (need).[1]

However, this frustration was different. This divine agitation was created by God and I could not resist it. This stirring was a "holy frustration." I knew that God had put a desire in me to accomplish more for Him and to have a closer relationship with Him. Like you, I wanted my life to "count" for the Kingdom. I wanted a deeper relationship with God. I desired a deeper intimacy with my wife and children. I wanted my ministry and work to take on a higher purpose.

In my search to understand this godly stirring in my life, I came across a book that fueled the fire already burning in my soul. This book literally changed the course of my life. It explained the agitation in my heart and created an "explanation" for what I was feeling. This book was *The God Chasers* by Tommy Tenney.[2] As I was reading Tommy's book in my prayer time early one morning, the glory of God filled my room. I started crying (with joy) as God poured out His love on me. After what seemed like hours of this outpouring, the Lord spoke to my heart, "Do you want to be a pastor of a local church or do you want to be a revivalist and transform your city for Me?" I was happy being a pastor of a local congregation, but I could not deny that the Lord had put this godly discontentment in my heart. I wanted my life to count for Him. I wanted more of God. So I quickly responded to God, "I want to be a revivalist!" At the time, I had no idea what a revivalist was. All I knew was I wanted "more" of God and I wanted my life to count for Him.

Re-Defining the Word Revival

Before I continue the story, I must first clear up some misconceptions about the meaning of the word *revival*. Growing up in the south as a Baptist, when I heard the word *revival*, I would think of a special speaker coming to our church for a series of meetings (i.e. evangelistic meetings). These gatherings would last about a week or so and then be over. Later in my life, I discovered in the Pentecostal and Charismatic camps, when one cries out for a revival, it takes on a different meaning. For example, when people are seeking revival in one of these camps, they simply mean that they desire more of God in their lives through the "outpouring of His Spirit." It is much more than a meeting. They seek an encounter with the living God.

These outpourings (revival meetings) produce physical healings, deliverance, and a "refreshing" from God. The emphasis of these meetings is on experiencing the presence of God (which produced these healings, deliverances, and refreshing moments) rather than salvation.

Both camps, the Baptist and the Pentecostal, were seeing a measure of God in their "revival" meetings, but one thing that I did not see in either setting were their cities being transformed. I did not see entire regions and nations repent and turn back to God. I did not see our culture changed in relationship to our schools, neighborhoods, and workplace. I simply did not see any long-lasting results in regards to these "revival" meetings. The impact on our cities was minimal, if any.

I am not saying that these meetings were ineffective or not ordained by God. However, in my heart, I knew God wanted to accomplish more through these revival meetings. I felt as if we were just scratching the surface of the magnitude of what God wanted to perform in our lives, cities, and regions. Even as a young boy, I knew that God had more in mind for us. But the question remained: Why was I feeling this emptiness and how could I experience more of God?

Searching for a God-ordained revival for our land, one day I looked up the word in a dictionary. The word *revival* comes from the word *revive*, which means "to return to life or consciousness" or "to bring back to use, attention, or popularity."[3] I do not know of a better definition of what God wants to do in the modern-day Church than "returning new life back into it" or "by bringing His Church back into the mainstream with new popularity and vigor." It is time for God's Church to regain respect and get power flowing into the mainstream of society. It is time for new life to be injected into the Body of Christ.

In the last years, we have seen many so-called revivals pop up all over the world. Some have been real and some have been counterfeit. In my pursuit of the real thing, I attended many revival meetings in America and throughout the world. I read almost every book on the subject of past and present revivals. In some of the revival meetings that I attended, I observed that God's presence was surely present. I saw physical healings take place. I saw people being set free from addictions (such as alcohol and drugs). I noticed lives being changed as they "soaked" under the power of God. Many were being changed and transformed. New life was being infused into people's lives and their churches. However, as I have already indicated, I observed that little impact was made on their cities. I noticed that the culture (workplace, schools, government buildings, etc.) was not affected. And after a few months had gone by, even the churches that had experienced revival had returned to "church as normal." In my heart, I cried out to God, "I know You want to do more!"

God Is Doing a New Thing

So as we use the term *revival* in this book, remember that I am not talking about a series of meetings when a special speaker preaches in our church. I am not talking about a meeting when God brings refreshing to a church. In this book, when I talk about the term *revival*, I am referring to God "pouring His Spirit" over an entire city or region where the whole region is impacted for God. I am relating how God is going outside the confines of our churches. I am talking about the believer buying groceries in the local supermarket and revival breaking out in the frozen food aisle. I am discussing what happens when one of God's saints delivers his mail to the local post office and revival breaks out as he waits in line. I am looking at what happens as the "saint" goes to work and revival breaks out in the lunchroom.

Every person in your city will either have to accept Jesus or reject Jesus, but everyone will hear about Him. This end-time revival must and will infiltrate every fiber of our lives—our schools, our neighborhoods, our workplaces, and even the place where we buy our groceries. Revival is coming, but it is nothing like the Body of Christ has seen before. God is doing a new thing! And this new thing is the coming revival emerging from the marketplace in this present-day marketplace movement.

There Was a Bump in the Road

With this new and enlarged perspective on the term *revival*, let me now continue with the rest of the story—my pursuit of true revival! After reading Tommy Tenney's book *The God Chasers*, I went to church the following Sunday and told my congregation about my encounter with God. I told them that we were going to "start believing" for this kind of revival for our region and that they were to expect to experience more of God in our services and lives. My first sermon on revival was called "There Was a Bump in the Road." That Sunday a change occurred in my life and church. Remember, at this time, I had a limited understanding of the full magnitude of what I meant when I said, "Let us believe for revival"; but at least my heart was open to God. All I knew at this time was that I wanted more of God in my life and I knew that God had more for me (like I know He has for you as well).

I discovered that not everyone shared the same excitement about "believing for revival." Within a year of our beginning to preach and teach on revival, about half of our church had left (maintaining tradition was more important). Let me make a quick statement. Whenever you pursue something from God, it will always cost you something. It might cost you a friendship, it might cost you time, it might cost you money even your life, but it will cost you something. Yes, the pursuit of revival had cost me a great deal. Your pursuit of revival will cost you a great deal, but let me also say this: "It is worth it!"

I knew that neither our church, nor I could turn back. The "revival bug" had bitten us! We were sick for God! Our only cure was for God to show up in a big way in our lives. We simply wanted more of God, not just for our church, but for our entire city. We would not be satisfied until God changed the spiritual climate of our city.

In my pursuit of revival, I attended almost every present-day revival site. I traveled to Florida, Canada, Illinois, Kansas, California, and Argentina. This preacher was hungry for more of God. As God touched me, His "refreshing" presence consumed my entire body. Tommy Tenney's book, *The God Chasers*, was the book God used in my life to jumpstart this entire process, but by now, I had read almost every book I could find on the subject of revival (over 50 books). I was so hungry for more of God. I was starving! I could not get enough of God and His love. God was so good! He put in me a new love for my family, my church, my city, and a new love for Jesus like I never had before. Wow!

God was such an awesome and loving God. Yes, revival is based in love. True revival will be an outpouring of His love on you. How do you know that God's end-time revival is for real? You will experience the love of God like you never have before!

Lord, I am hungry for more of Your love. God, I am hungry for the "real thing."

You Never Ask Me "How"

In our local church, we started a special prayer meeting as we started believing for revival. Like many other churches, we had done everything we knew to do to bring revival to our church and region. After about two years of praying, preaching and believing for revival (we were getting discouraged waiting on God), God spoke to my heart and asked me a second question (that was another life-changing experience). He said, "Marcus, you asked Me for revival, but you never asked Me *how* revival would come."

When God asks you a question, believe me, He already knows the answer, but He wants you to know. I responded, "How, Lord?" The Lord spoke again, "Revival is coming to the marketplace, to the sports arenas, the government buildings, the media, the music studios. I want you to take My love to your city. I want My power to transform your city with the love of My Son, Jesus. Will you do that for Me, son?"

I shouted out loud, "That's it! Now I know how God will bring revival to our city, region, and nation." It will not be *in* the church building, but *through* the Church as we take Jesus outside the perimeters of the building. The Church is not the building, but the Church is the people. You are the Church! We will take Church to them (the lost). We have been waiting for the lost to come to the church, but we have missed the mark. We were called to take the Church to the lost. We must be sent out as revivalists—taking the love of Jesus to our workplaces, our schools, and the sports arenas. We must take Jesus to our cities. We must take Jesus to the world!

At this time my mind was racing, totally out of control! I now knew that God wanted me to look deeper into what He meant when He said, "Revival is coming to the marketplace!" God had showed me the missing element, the method of *how* He desired for revival to come. I immediately started re-reading the Bible with my "new spiritual glasses" that enabled me to see God bringing revival to the marketplace. I read the Bible with the marketplace in mind. New revelation flooded my heart. It was though I was reading the Bible for the first time (even though I had read it through many times before).

I read about the 12 apostles, who were primarily all marketplace leaders. The original twelve followers of Christ had business backgrounds. They were not priests in the church, but workers in the marketplace. They worked hard in their jobs (like most of you). As I continued to re-read the Bible, I observed that the majority of the miracles performed by the disciples and Jesus were performed outside the borders of the church. The majority of the people touched by Jesus were touched not in the local church, but in the marketplace. Jesus and His disciples were not just "Sunday Christians," but "24/7" Christians. What they taught, they lived Monday through Saturday (not just on Sunday). Being a marketplace minister was a lifestyle; not just something they talked about on Sunday (or Saturday, in Jesus' days at the synagogue).

One day the Holy Spirit reminded me that Jesus Himself was a businessman at one stage of His life. Like some of His disciples, Jesus was part of a family business. For Jesus it was carpentry and for some of the others it was a fishing business. Jesus worked hard daily in His business until the age of 30. For 30 years, Jesus was trained for His future ministry working in a business, not in the synagogue (church). In my heart, I was getting so excited! I was seeing things in the Bible that had always been there, but God, through the Holy Spirit, was now allowing me to see how future revival was coming—not just *to* the marketplace, but *from* the marketplace. Revival had already taken place in the times of Jesus and in the first church in the Book of Acts, but now God was about to repeat Himself. God always saves the best for last—your generation.

Again God spoke to my heart…

"My end-time revival is about to come from the marketplace. My end-time Church will experience an even greater measure of My power and anointing. With the end-time outpouring of My Spirit, all segments of society will be touched by My glory, especially the marketplace."

I am not advocating anything new, but what I am advocating is that God is doing something new in His Church. He is showing us how the Church was meant to function in the world. He wants us to reevaluate how our churches measure up to the first church in the Book of Acts. He desires us to ask ourselves the hard question…how effective are we in taking our city and world for Christ? It is time we work smarter rather than harder. It is time we work *with* God, not *against* Him, utilizing *His* methods for winning the world. Even though I was so excited with this new perspective, I knew that something was still missing. I needed the missing parts to put the "the whole puzzle together." Once again, God was faithful. The next piece of the puzzle, was the book, *God@Work*, written by my new friend Rich Marshall.[4]

The Pieces of the Puzzle Falling in Place

The Lord impressed upon me to take my wife to a meeting with Dr. Bill Hamon in Florida. Christian International was hosting a business conference, and the keynote speaker was a Californian named Rich Marshall. Rich was teaching from his new book, *God@Work*. Once the meeting was about to start, my spirit was waiting eagerly with anticipation, even though I did not know who Rich Marshall was or his topic. However, I knew that God was about to reveal something new that would give me further direction and clarity in my search.

Rich spoke about how God was about to transform our cities by releasing marketplace ministers. He challenged each one of us in the audience to start "re-thinking" how we do church in relationship to the marketplace. Rich spoke about all of us being in "full-time" ministry, both the pastor and layman. About halfway through the meeting, I nudged my wife and said, "Honey, it is all coming together now. I think we have found the missing piece of the puzzle."

I glanced at my wife sitting next to me. By now, we both had tears in our eyes. However, these were tears of joy, not sadness. My wife, Sharon, leaned over to me and said with a whisper, "Aren't you glad we obeyed God and came to this meeting?" I kissed her on her check and responded, "Yes, Honey!"

God was leading us one step closer to understanding His "heartbeat" in relation to this end-time revival that will consume all America and the world. We were now beginning to understand not only that revival was coming, but also *how* revival would come: *from the marketplace!* This was another crossroad moment in our lives.

The Power of Divine Connections

God had used the book, *The God Chasers*, to help me launch my quest for seeing "true revival" transform every town, city, and region in America and around the world. Then, God used the book, *God@Work*, by Rich Marshall to help me understand how it will be accomplished: from the marketplace. Allow me to make this one key point before moving on: *Do not underestimate the power of God's Word and the books written by anointed men and women of God. They can become divine connections in your life.*

When I speak about the power of divine connections, I do not mean I necessarily have to have a lifelong friendship with someone in order to be impacted. I did have the pleasure of meeting Tommy Tenney at a book signing in Canada; and I personally came to know Rich Marshall when he came to speak in our church. Yes, I wish I could spend more time getting to know these two men; however, God used their books to change my life, not necessarily their personal contact.

I have met so many people who want to be "close" to this person or that person. In a similar fashion many come to me and communicate their desire for a closer walk with Jesus. I say to these individuals, "If you want to feel closer to Him, then spend more time with Him in His Word."

Would you like to fly all over the world and meet the many men and women whom God is using today to change the lives of so many? You know what—you can! By picking up their books and reading about their journeys, you will have the opportunity of sitting down with them in the living room of their hearts.

Having written several books, I know how long it takes to write a book: the research time, the preparation time and time alone with God. One may read a book in a few days, but the time it took to discover the truths in that book probably encompassed 50 years of someone's life, including life experiences and the wisdom gained from those experiences. Yes, God can use anointed books as divine connections to literally change the course of your life.

I pray that this book will create a divine connection for you and that it will "spark a fire" in your soul that will engulf you and cause you to become hungrier for more of God. It is my desire that you will discover your role in God's modern-day marketplace movement. I pray that a new desire will begin to form within you and that you will come to know God's end-time plan for His Church and the role you will play. I trust that you will take God Factor into your workplace, *getting the edge* you need to succeed in life.

The pursuit of revival is a lifelong process. One never arrives, for you are constantly pursuing God in new ways. The quest for knowledge and wisdom is never ceasing. So let us pursue God and His will for our lives, cities, and regions. If you are hungry and long to know more about God's end-time plan for His Church, then get ready. The best is yet ahead!

A Book List for Your Help

Because books have been such an important element of my life, I have a book list in the appendix. These are titles that I believe will be helpful to you. Some of my readers are already well versed in this subject matter. The list is not all-inclusive, but

I hope it will be helpful to you as you pursue God and His end-time revival that is coming. The Marketplace movement is upon us, and I trust that you will find your place within this great move of God.

Now I Know the How

Once I discovered how revival was about to hit our city from the marketplace, I started reading as many books as I could find regarding the relationship between God and the marketplace. I discovered that many books had been written on this subject. However, several of these books had been published years ago. As I talked to some of these publishing companies, they informed me that the titles were starting to sell again. One publishing company informed me that one of its books was now selling like it had when it was first released.

The Holy Spirit reminded me once again of the reason. He spoke to my heart, "God is pouring out His Spirit onto His Body for His saints to get understanding in what God is about to do in the near future." Continuing my search, I discovered many new books on God and the marketplace. I was amazed at the volume of information. This only further confirmed in my heart that I was on the right track. It was much like what happens when you buy a car, thinking you own the only one of that make and model. But then you notice the same kind of car almost everywhere. This truth was right before my eyes all along, but it was not God's timing. But praise God! For now it is the time! The floodgates have been opened to my heart and all I can see around me is "God and the marketplace." As God has revealed transcendent truth to me, God wants to reveal it to you. I believe that God has saved His best "movement" for last. God is saving His best for you!

Endnotes

1. Philippians 4:11.

2. Tommy Tenney, *The God Chasers* (Shippensburg, Pennsylvania: Destiny Image, 1999).

3. Victoria Neufeldt, *Webster's New World Dictionary* (New York, New York: Warner Books, 1990), 505.

4. Rich Marshall, *God@Work* (Shippensburg, Pennsylvania: Destiny Image, 2000).

Chapter 2

DISCOVERING YOUR IDENTITY

Wherefore also we pray always for you, that our God would count you worthy of this calling, and fulfil all the good pleasure of His goodness, and the work of faith with power (2 Thessalonians 1:11).

Now that I was on the journey, I started reading and praying for more understanding on this coming move of God. I wanted to understand the purposes of God, and it was at this time that God brought an explosion in my spirit. I had found *why* I had been born. In my prayer time the Lord reminded me why I was both a businessman and a pastor, that my education background was both in business and in theological school. The pieces of the puzzle were all coming together. I was discovering my identity!

Some of you may be in the process of discovering your identity as well. I want to encourage you to continue in your pursuit. For when you discover and begin to activate your life's calling, the years of waiting and the numerous disappointments will all begin to make sense. Now is not the time to quit. Press forward, until you apprehend your calling and see your dreams transformed into reality.

I will talk further about this later, but let me make one quick point in regard to your identity. First, you must know your identity in relationship to Christ and secondly, you must know your identity in relationship to your calling. Your identity has to do with your preparation for your calling. Your calling has to do with the divine purpose and plans for your life here on earth. Discovering your identity is key to your success in life.

For example, a fish cannot swim on land because a fish was called to live in the water. If a fish stays out of water too long, it will die. Likewise, you cannot be successful outside of your calling. Many Christians are in the wrong environment, trying to succeed. Like a fish trying to live on land, you cannot succeed if you are in the wrong place. If you will simply jump back in the water (your calling), then success will be a part of your life once again.

It Is Not the Devil

Many Christians think that their slow progress is because the devil is hindering them. Yes, the devil can hinder your progress, but many times your progress is hindered because you are not walking in your calling. Simply, you have not discovered your true identity. God is so good! God would rather let you fail at your good ideas (your will) than let you miss the best for your life. For many of you, your failure might be the best thing that could happen to you. How could that be?

God always wants the best for His children. He wants you to discover the gifts He has deposited in you. He will allow you to fail, because He desires to transfer you from the environment you have created for yourself and cause you to walk in the calling that He has created for you. Like a good father, God wants you to be all you can be as you walk in your God-given identity. Isn't that what a good father would do? God deeply desires for you to discover your purpose and identity in life. Life is more than getting your name written in the Lamb's Book of Life; life is also about discovering and walking in your God-ordained purpose and identity. Too many of us stop at the door of salvation and never get around to fulfilling our destiny.

I remember how God led me to my lovely wife, Sharon. As a Christian single, I felt the need of being with someone at all times of my life. Looking back now, I realize that I was afraid to be alone. I desperately needed to be with someone. One day the Lord spoke to my heart, "Marc, I want you to stop dating and begin to trust Me." As I obeyed the Lord, the next six months of my life seemed like eternity. I stopped dating, but it was hard for me to be alone. Eventually, because of my obedience, I was introduced to my beautiful wife, Sharon, while I was attending a Christian meeting in Florida. For God to introduce me to my wife, the best for me, I had to let go of my previous relationships, which were second best.

Your Failure Versus Your Success

Your failure just might be the path to your success. God never causes us to fail to hurt us. God allows us to fail so we may discover the best He has for our life. Our failures are not final; they are simply doorways into God's designed plans for us. Success is not based on your failure, but on how you respond to failure. Many times God is speaking to us through life's trials and errors. How we respond to these trials and errors will determine our success in life. One can only truly fail if one quits.

Like you, I am tired of just working hard. I want to work smart and not hard. I want to walk in the "calling" God has for me. I want to discover my identity. How about you? Are you ready for a change? Are you ready to discover your "dual" calling as a saint? Are you ready to achieve your true success?

Break-Out Time

Finding your identity is a lifelong process, but when you finally discover it, watch out—this is when life really begins!

How do you know when you have discovered your identity? You can know that you have made the discovery when you begin to walk in your God-ordained assignment in life. At that moment success will break out on all sides of your life. The needed money will suddenly appear for that project you have worked so hard to accomplish. The people who have been assigned to you will emerge. The work you were assigned to accomplish will be made clear in your mind. All the necessary ingredients to achieve your calling will now be made available to you. Instead of being tolerated, you will now be celebrated. Yes, you will know it! For your life will never be the same once you discover and walk in your identity and your calling.

Your "Dual" Calling

*And hath made us **kings and priests** unto God and His Father; to Him be glory and dominion for ever and ever. Amen* (Revelation 1:6, emphasis added).

It is critical for you to discover your identity in Christ and your identity in God's will for your life on this earth. But according to Revelation 1:6, it is also essential that each Christian understand that he has two assignments (dual calling) to fulfill. You are called to walk as a "priest" and a "king" in this world. We will devote entire chapters to discussing the roles of the priest and king, but let me tell you right now—success in your Christian walk will be determined by how you fulfill both of your callings—as a priest and king. The priestly anointing (*marketplace ministers*) represents your call to the ministry, and your kingly anointing (*marketplace managers*) represents your call to be a steward of God's finances in the marketplace. You are both full-time priests (men and women) and full-time kings (men and women). The day of the clergy being thought of as the only full-time ministry must come to an end. We all are called to be full-time ministers whether we serve Him behind the pulpit or behind a desk, in a hospital, on a job site, or wherever God has you.

Finding Your Place

As the Lord allows me to speak to audiences around the world, one of the greatest joys I have is seeing people discover their identities. Businessmen and women come up to me after a meeting with tears in their eyes, expressing joy because they have discovered that they are called to be the "pastors" of their businesses as well as financial managers. Senior pastors of churches grab me by the arm and thank me for helping them understand the full calling of the businessmen and women of their church. Stay-at-home moms express their joy in realizing that they are significant in God's Kingdom as they learn how to be "priests and kings" in their homes and in their neighborhoods. Students take me to the side and tell me how their lives have changed, now that they realize their "dual" roles as students and as missionaries at school.

Once you find your place and calling in God's family, then you look at life with a whole new perspective. Your workplace becomes a ministry opportunity. Your neighborhood becomes a new harvest field. Your school becomes a mission field. Your social group becomes a place to share Christ. Life takes on a whole new meaning.

We have heard the phrase "prosperity with purpose"; now we have the new phrase "the marketplace with a mission." Monday morning becomes the time to enter your own mission field. Instead of dreading Mondays, you are beginning a new week full of opportunities to influence others for the Kingdom of God. It becomes a matter of seeing your glass half-full or half-empty. It is all how you look at your circumstances. Sunday is your *training* ground, but Monday is your *sharing* ground. Move out this next Monday and walk in your "dual calling" as both kings (*marketplace managers*) and priests (*marketplace ministers*).

Joseph Discovered His Identity

Joseph was a man with an identity crisis. But in a single day he went from the prison to the palace, and his life immediately changed. Joseph discovered why he had been born. Joseph realized who he was in God's plan. Joseph found his identity. From being sold into slavery by his brothers, to his betrayal by Potiphar's wife, to interpreting the Pharaoh's dreams while in prison, Joseph finally understood why God had taken him down this path of life. It was finally all making sense.

Does your life make sense? God told you that you would be on top of the mountain, but all your life the only vision you have had of the mountain is from the valley below. Well, be encouraged by Joseph's life. Trust God that He is directing your life in every "valley situation." Every "valley experience" is bringing you one step closer to reaching the top of your mountain. Yes, you will discover your "dual calling" in life, and life will never be the same. Your life is about to change! God is calling you to be both a "king and priest" for the Kingdom of God. He needs you! You are important to His plans and purposes for this next movement— the marketplace movement!

One of my reasons for writing this book is to help each believer recognize the "dual calling" on his or her life. God is about to bring a great harvest of souls to His Church, but in order for His Church to pull in the great harvest nets, we must understand that everyone (the whole Body of Christ) is needed. Not one person will be left out of God's plan for His end-time harvest.

God is calling you! He is calling you to the marketplace as both a king and a priest!

Chapter 3

CALLED TO THE MARKETPLACE

And the saying pleased the whole multitude: and they chose Stephen, a man full of faith and of the Holy Ghost, and Philip, and Prochorus, and Nicanor, and Timon, and Parmenas, and Nicolas a proselyte of Antioch: whom they set before the apostles: and when they had prayed, they laid their hands on them. And the word of God increased; and the number of the disciples multiplied in Jerusalem greatly; and a great company of the priests were obedient to the faith. And Stephen, full of faith and power, did great wonders and miracles among the people (Acts 6:5-8).

The Church of the 21st century is in a transition period. Many ministry leaders are "rethinking" the way they do church. If we are going to get the God Factor working in our lives, we must reevaluate the way we do things. Many pastors are asking, "Does what I am doing line up with God's Word? How can I be more effective and reach more with the message of Christ?"

As we learn more about what God is doing in this new marketplace movement, I believe the answers to these questions will become increasingly clear. Before we go much further exploring how God is moving into the marketplace, let us first define what we mean when we talk about the term *marketplace.*

The Marketplace: A Broader View

You have already discovered what God meant when He said, "I will pour out My Spirit upon all flesh." I believe God was saying that He is about to bring "true revival" to the world. We have established that God's end-time revival will be like nothing else the Body of Christ has seen. The "how" of revival is about to emerge not from the local church (nuclear church), but from the marketplace (extended church).

As I was praying, the Lord spoke these words, "You are thinking too small. When I speak of the marketplace, I am referring to all segments of society, not just the workplace. My end-time revival will affect everyone. Remember, I will pour out My spirit upon all flesh (the saved and the unsaved)."

Recently, at a marketplace leaders' conference in Dallas, Texas, I noticed in our roundtable discussion sessions that each person had a different understanding of the term *marketplace*. One person used it in relation to buying one's groceries at a local supermarket. Another used it to describe "a place where the stock market exists (i.e. Wall Street)." Some defined the word *marketplace* as just the workplace, the location were we spend the majority of our time each week. As a matter of fact, all these definitions are correct.

However, in this book, when I use the term *marketplace*, I am using the term in its broader perspective. I am not just referring to the workplace or the business setting. I am referring to the great world around us where men and women interact in the daily transactions of life outside the four walls of the nuclear church (Sunday). The marketplace is the "everyday world of man" that the Church is trying to reach. It is where we buy our groceries. It is where we go to work. It is where we trade, do business, and carry out economic affairs.

For example, God's end-time revival in the marketplace might change the way our government functions, as God pours out His Spirit on government workers and officials. God's end-time revival in the marketplace might influence an NFL football game on Sunday afternoon, because we will change the way we think of sports and sports figures. Television programs like MTV might stop the broadcast of the top ten music videos to announce that God broke out in a local concert. Media personalities might repent right on a television program for presenting the gospel incorrectly. Schools that have tried to keep God out by banning school prayer will now gladly welcome Him back, as students and teachers alike are consumed by the power of God. Workplace coffee rooms will be converted to Bible meeting areas, as the CEOs of many companies will have dramatic conversion experiences.

Neighborhood housewives' Bible studies, which once had just a few in attendance, will now be filled to capacity as God's revival power descends upon an entire neighborhood. Local shopping centers will become revival centers as God's power descends upon the checkout clerks. The marketplace is not just the workplace, but God's power being poured out upon all flesh—*our workplaces, our schools, our neighborhoods, our government buildings, and our sports arenas. All flesh will be touched by this present-day Marketplace movement!*

When I state that revival is coming from the marketplace, I am declaring that God is moving outside of the restrictions of the church to permeate every aspect of society. From the media, music, government, education, business, the workplace, neighborhoods, etc....God is about to "pour out His Spirit upon all flesh." The Marketplace movement is about God's power not just touching the local church, but reshaping our culture. This new movement is about city transformation. It is about God's love reaching out to the whole world.

Paradigm Shift

When God wants to do something new, sometimes He first must "frustrate" your current plans. Why? Your present success may be the biggest obstacle to your discovering God's new plan for your life. For example, churches today are excited if they have a hundred new converts in a given year. Spiritual leaders who have a church of a thousand members think they are being effective for Christ. But how effective are we being? It is sad to say, but the Church is losing the battle. Our largest churches in America represent only about one percent of the world's population. Can we really brag about our effectiveness? There must be a better way!

When the progress of a certain business begins to slow down, a good leader reevaluates his efforts. God is frustrating the plans of many church leaders around the world to get them to seek the face of God. He is resisting their efforts, slowing down their progress as He tries to get them to see that a shift in His plans is taking place. God has a new method for reaping His end-time harvest, but we must start lining up with this plan. What is God's new plan? God's new plan is to take back the marketplace for Christ. God is not just taking back the finances for His Kingdom, but God is taking back the souls as well (the world's marketplace leaders).

In Acts 6, we read that the early church had a problem. The widows of the day needed assistance. Their physical needs had created a great controversy for the church. In an effort to bring a positive solution to this problem, the apostles chose men from the church to help resolve the situation. The unique aspect of this story was not only *how* Stephen (the businessman) was chosen to help feed the widows, but also that when Stephen went to purchase the bread, the "wonders and miracles" followed him. Stephen, the businessman (a marketplace leader) was now acting as a minister (*marketplace minister*) like the apostles. Stephen was not an apostle, but *only* a deacon. Stephen was not in "full-time" ministry. Stephen was *only* a businessman. If he were in one of our churches today, Stephen may have been made to feel like a second-class citizen, because he was not in full-time ministry. He was *only* a businessman whose main duty was to provide for the financial needs of his church. He was not qualified to minister like the other full-time apostles.

Why is this story in the Bible so important? It is important because it supplies clues as to how God wants to work in our days. God had "expanded" His power, from the original 12 apostles to others like Stephen who were ordinary businessmen. However, these ordinary businessmen were not ordinary to God. Stephen was important to God's plan for the early church.

Likewise, you are important in God's plan for the end-time harvest that is taking place in the marketplace. The modern-day Church is in a paradigm shift. The word *paradigm* means "an example or model."[1] The word *shift* means "to move from one person or place to another."[2] *The paradigm shift taking place is God transferring His anointing to now be placed upon **all saints**, regardless of their status in life. God has determined that He will reach the marketplaces of the world through those who* *work in those places.* This paradigm shift is exciting! Why? It is thrilling because God is about to recruit His entire Church to participate in His end-time harvest of souls. Are you excited yet? You should be because God must really love you! Why would I say that? God in His love and mercy is recruiting *you* to participate in His end-time harvest from the marketplace. He could use His angels to get the job done, but He loves you so much that He is giving everyone who responds to the call the opportunity to take part in this end-time harvest. Jesus said, "Many are called, but few are chosen."[3] I believe He was referring to the marketplace call. How will you respond?

> *Then saith He unto His disciples, The harvest truly is plenteous, but the labourers are few; pray ye therefore the Lord of the harvest, that He will send forth labourers into His harvest* (Matthew 9:37-38).

God is about to alleviate the "shortage of labor" problem in His worldwide plan. He is now recruiting the whole Church to assist Him in the completion of this enormous task. God is not only recruiting workers within the church but He is also harvesting new workers from the marketplace, to which we are called. The Church is in a time of transition. A paradigm shift has begun. Are you ready?

Are you ready to be used by God? Are you now able to see that your job is your ministry? Are you beginning to see the school you attend as God's harvest field? Have you realized that the neighborhood you live in is the place where God wants to break out next? The Church is about to work smarter (God's way) and not harder (man's way).

What will be the "tool" that God will use, not only to pull in the harvest, but also to train and equip the laborers?

Endnotes

1. Kenneth Kister, *Webster's New World Dictionary* (New York, New York: Warner Books, 1990), 426.

2. Kenneth Kister, *Webster's New World Dictionary*, 542.

3. Matthew 22:14.

Chapter 4

GOD'S ESTABLISHED CHURCH

And I say also unto thee, That thou art Peter, and upon this rock I will build My church; and the gates of hell shall not prevail against it (Matthew 16:18).

Even though God's modern-day Church is in a state of transition, she is still the "tool" God will use to pull in His end-time harvest of souls. Remember that the Church is not a building, it is a living organism. It is the Body of Christ. I believe that the end-time Church will have *great power, great grace, and great provision* (finances). It will not be lacking in one single thing. The Church will be the primary weapon used by God to take back the wealth of the world. It is this wealth that will be used to fund God's end-time harvest originating from the marketplace.

The Church will also be the primary tool used by God to train the laborers (harvesters) who will be sent into the harvest fields (the marketplace). Why am I making such an issue about the Church? Simply, we cannot miss the mechanism through which God will work to accomplish His purposes and plans. If you have committed your life to Christ, then you are the Church. Yes, God's Church has not yet fully arrived. It is far from being perfect. We might not be there yet, but we are moving in the right direction. We are beginning to see present-day "wonders and miracles" in the marketplace. We are seeing modern-day churches "properly handle great amounts of wealth" for the Kingdom of God. The modern-day Church is not starting from ground zero. In fact, the process of restoration that started so many centuries ago is speeding up in our generation.

God's Church Is Being Restored

God is restoring His Church back to its original power and glory! What is this thing we call the restoration process? First of all, I want to say that God's Church is already established to some degree. The problem is that we are not yet walking in its "fullness." To be more accurate—God's Church is in the process of *being* established. What I mean is that God's Church is being restored from one generation to the next. After the beginnings of the church that we read about in the Book of Acts, the church went through a period for about five hundred years of "silence" when much was lost and it became corrupted. Since that period, through many courageous men and women during different periods of time, God has been restoring the Church back to its "fullness" as the first church in the Book of Acts.

To prepare God's people for works of service, so that the body of Christ may be built up until we all reach unity in the faith and in the knowledge of the Son of God and become mature, attaining to the whole measure of the fullness of Christ (Ephesians 4:12-13 NIV).

In the first church, Peter preached and three thousand souls were saved in a single service. In Peter's *shadow*, the power of God was present to heal the sick. Many in the church sold what they had and gave the proceeds to the poor. Ananias and Sapphira fell dead under the power of the Holy Spirit.[1] Sadly, much of that power and influence was lost as the church turned the corner into the second century. In the last six hundred years we have watched as God has been reversing the curses of religion and preparing the Church for this very hour. We live in a day when the Church is being restored as we walk back into its "full power."

The Restoration Process

One may ask, "What process of restoration has God used in the past until the present time? How will God restore back to the Church this great power, great grace, and great provision?" One of the most renowned of the reformers was a man named Martin Luther. His message that we are "saved by grace" set a blaze of reformation fires in Germany and gave impetus to the birth of the Protestant Movement in the 16th century. The primary emphasis of Luther and the other reformers was that we are "justified by faith," not works. The name Lutheran

Church was a nickname fastened upon the followers of Martin Luther. Emerging out of the fires of reformation came the Anabaptists, who had discovered the truth of holiness and baptism by immersion. From this group we have the birth of various denominations.

In the 17th century we observe the launch of the Holiness movement. Such leaders as John Wesley and Charles Whitfield are recognized as the fiery preachers of those times. The Methodists, as they were eventually called, proclaimed the message of sanctification. One step at a time God was restoring the lost treasures of the early church.

As we round the corner into the beginning of the 20th century a movement known as the Pentecostal movement meets us. One of the Pentecostals' defining messages was the restoration of the "baptism of the Holy Spirit." One of the biggest events of this era was the 1906 Azusa Street Revival in Los Angeles. God moved in a miraculous way as blacks, whites, rich, poor, male, female, young and old all came together to see and feel the power of God. To this day, many meetings take on the name "Azusa" as a symbolic gesture of this event. In his book, *The Eternal Church*, Bill Hamon recounts:

> A former student of Parham's, who had been a Baptist minister and was now a southern Negro Holiness preacher was the instrument God used to escalate this truth. During three years of continuous Pentecostal revival at Azusa Street people came from all over the world to discover what new things God had wrought. It was carried by the news media and brought to the attention of the world.[2]

With the Pentecostal movement also came an emphasis on the neglected gifts of the Spirit: the gifts of utterance (tongues and prophecy), gifts of revelation (word of knowledge and word of wisdom), and gifts of power (healing and working of miracles). Other leaders emerged during those times—like Aimee Semple McPherson, who was used mightily in the area of physical healings.

Denominations like the Assemblies of God and Foursquare Churches also were birthed.

Next in the unfolding restoration came the Latter Rain movement around the 1940s. The activation of prophecy became a major emphasis during this time. During this movement, high praise became popular with the churches. Ministries started recognizing the importance of the fivefold ministry gifts. Before this time you were identified either as an evangelist or a pastor. But now with the "ascension gifts" being restored, leaders were recognized as teachers, pastors, evangelists, prophets, or apostles.

After the Latter Rain movement came the Charismatic movement in the late 1950s and early 1960s. With this movement came a renewed emphasis on "speaking in tongues," "the gifts of the Spirit," and the "laying on of hands." Thousands in many denominations were powerfully influenced by this move of the Spirit. The emphasis on "laying on of hands" reestablished more healing, as well as prophetic activation and deliverance from demons.

In the 1970s, we watched the emergence of what some have called the Prosperity, Faith, and Word movement. Oral Roberts was one of the earlier proponents of healing and faith. Who can forget his telling us that God is a good God and desires Christians to be in health and prosper even as their souls prosper?

In the 1980s came the Prophetic movement with the restoration of the office of the prophet and gift of prophecy to the Body of Christ. In the 1990s came the Unity of the Church movement and the Apostolic movement. In these present times we have watched the birth of many movements simultaneously taking place—the Prayer movement, the City Transformation movement, the Women's movement, the Marketplace movement (a.k.a. the Saints movement).

It is interesting and important to note that each new movement builds upon the last one. The last emphasis of God does not end, but simply evolves into the next one. Each restoration movement has significance and must never be forgotten. But we must also remember that the process is not complete and we must continue to move forward.

This has been God's restoration process throughout the history of the church. God has been restoring His Church over the last two thousand years, moving it closer and closer to its original plan and purpose. It is also important to note that during the last 50 years in the Church restoration process, not only does one movement build upon another, but with each new movement God releases more grace upon His Church. This grace is essential to the Church's fulfilling the Great Commission (See Mt. 28:19-20). With the Marketplace movement, the Body of Christ will experience God's outpouring of His grace like it has never witnessed before! Not only will we see more men and women added to the Kingdom than at any other time in our church history, but more Christians will be used in this next movement than ever before. The entire Body of Christ will be used and trained to pull in this end-time harvest from the marketplace. God is saving the Marketplace movement to be *the best ever*!

Unfortunately, history has proven to us that as one movement of God was built upon the prior movement, the transition was not always smooth. Many times, the leaders of the last movement will become the greatest enemies of the next movement. Human nature has a tendency to hold tightly to the old methods (last movement) rather than move into the new dimensions of restoration. Simply, we do not like change. If God's end-time Church is going to achieve any measure of success, then we must be willing to "walk" with God. We cannot live in the past (old movements), but we have to live in the present (new movements of God).

The Church Is Being Transformed

What is the purpose to this little review of history? We must see the Church as a progressing, changing, and ever-evolving living organism. The Church is being transformed from day to day, from one generation to the next! We have not yet arrived to God's fullness, but we are getting closer. Not only will the end-time

Church be fully restored, but I also believe we will walk in an even greater power and anointing.

> *Verily, verily, I say unto you, He that believeth on Me, the works that I do shall he do also; and greater works than these shall he do; because I go unto My Father (John 14:12).*

It is my prayer that the Church in this generation will experience a new power and anointing that no past move of God has ever experienced. As we faithfully take the gospel to the marketplace, let's believe that we will see with our natural eyes God's power accompanying our faith.

One question still remains. What will it take for God's end-time Church to walk in its "fullness"? What must the Church accomplish before God will release His power and anointing to walk in the supernatural? Is there something we still are not doing? Is the Church still walking in its "old revelation"? Or is it that God is waiting on His Church to "turn directions" and start focusing on—the marketplace?

Great Power, Great Grace, and Great Provision

> *And with **great power** gave the apostles witness of the resurrection of the Lord Jesus: and **great grace** was upon them all. **Neither was there any among them that lacked:** for as many as were possessors of lands or houses sold them, and brought the prices of the things that were sold, and laid them down at the apostles' feet: and distribution was made unto every man according as he had need (Acts 4:33-35, emphasis added).*

The early church experienced great power, great grace, and great provision.

As we have seen throughout church history, God has been in the background working to restore His Church to its "fullness" with all the original power, glory, and provision. Although fivefold ministry gifts are in varying stages of restoration, something seems to still be lacking. Unlike the first church, we are still not walking in the full magnitude (power, grace, and provision) of what God has for His present-day Church. It is my conviction that one of the things that must happen is the Church must lift her eyes and look beyond the programs and events that captivate her attention inside the structure of the church. She must begin to see that there is a great battle for the souls of men, and one of the places where that battle is taking place is in—the marketplace! We can be confident that as we take up the challenge of reaching out into the marketplace, God will honor us with great grace.

Every successful corporate structure must have a mission statement that describes its place in the world. What is the Church's mission statement?

The Church Mission Statement

And Jesus came and spake unto them, saying, All power is given unto Me in heaven and in earth. Go ye therefore [into the marketplace], *and teach all nations, baptizing them in the name of the Father, and of the Son, and of the Holy Ghost: teaching them to observe all things whatsoever I have commanded you: and, lo, I am with you always, even unto the end of the world* (Matthew 28:18-20).

To fulfill this mission statement, the Church must change its direction and start focusing on the harvest—from the marketplace. Secondly, the Church must trust God to meet her every need as she responds to the call and seeks to effectively impact the surrounding culture with the provisions supplied by the Lord. From their ranks will emerge men and women with a kingly call who will greatly and directly impact the business culture. I believe that the favor of God will be upon these *marketplace managers (kingly call)*, and they will tap into great financial resources for the Kingdom. And thirdly, the Church must train the "saints" to pull in the harvest—*marketplace ministers*. Yes, God is releasing great grace, power, and provision to finish the job—The Great Commission—the mission statement of the Church!

Next, let's see specifically how the marketplace prophets and the marketplace apostles will be used to bring in God's end-time harvest from the marketplace.

Endnotes

1. Acts 5:1-10.

2. Dr. Bill Hamon, *The Eternal Church* (Phoenix, Arizona: Christian International Publishing, 1982), 213.

Chapter 5

LEADERSHIP SHIFT

And He gave some, apostles; and some, prophets; and some, evangelists; and some, pastors and teachers; for the perfecting of the saints, for the work of the ministry, for the edifying of the body of Christ (Ephesians 4:11-12).

For some of my readers, the use of the terms, *apostle* and *prophet* may cause division within the ranks. There are many who believe these ministries no longer exist. However, according to Paul's words to the church at Ephesus, these ministries are critical for equipping God's people so that they can do the work they are called to do. As God is restoring all fivefold ministry offices, we must understand we are not interested in creating new titles, but we are interested in discovering the *functions* the offices have within the Body of Christ. We want to explore how the fivefold ministry can assist you in becoming all you can be in Christ. With my strong evangelical background, I had to wrestle with these issues myself, for I was one of those who believed these ministries no longer existed. However, as I pursued God and continued to read His Word, I soon realized that I needed the support of all fivefold offices to walk in the fullness of Christ.

Restoring New Leaders

And are built upon the foundation of the apostles and prophets, Jesus Christ Himself being the chief corner stone (Ephesians 2:20).

God's priests (*marketplace ministers*) must be set in place not only to pull in the harvest from the marketplace, but also to train the new converts as well. The apostles and prophets governed the first church. Likewise, God's end-time Church will have the same divine order, power, authority, and resources. When Paul said *"first,"* he meant *first*. *"First apostles and prophets, and Jesus Christ being the chief cornerstone."*[1] Jesus is our CEO, and He has set apostles and prophets as His chief administrators to train men and women to accomplish the tasks He has established.

I believe that it is important that we experience the emergence of true apostles and prophets who are able to spiritually oversee the blessings God desires to bring into the Church. These people must be men and women who have an understanding of the full purposes of God and who will not "harvest" these finances for themselves and their pet projects. It will probably take a new generation of leaders who understand God's heart for the poor and the socially disenfranchised. They will not waste God's blessings on inordinate buildings or irrelevant and ineffective programs. Their passion will beat in tune with the heart of the Father. As we move forward to the "fullness" God designed, we must "let God be God." We cannot take any man-made shortcuts that bypass God's ways and overlook His methods.

The Joseph/Daniel Company

In God's first church, God had only a few apostles and prophets, but in God's end-time Church, He is restoring a "company" of believers who will walk in the apostolic and prophetic anointing. I call this company the "Joseph/Daniel Company." God is expanding His anointing from the original 12 apostles to thousands, even millions, of Christians in the years to come. We in the western world have a very small concept of the great power that God is manifesting in other parts of the world. If we see a "miracle" here in the western culture we tend to make such a great deal about this event when in reality these sort of miracles are everyday occurrences for our brothers and sisters in the third world. For many years they have been flowing in the "greater works" of Jesus as He has multiplied His power through these saints. As we begin to align ourselves with God's agenda in these days and allow faith to be built into us by the power of the Holy Spirit, then the "greater works" anointing will start to flow in our midst.[2] God not only wants to release great power, great grace, and great provision back into the Church with the restoration of both the prophet and apostle, but also a "greater works" anointing. What is the purpose of this new power? Simply, it is to convince the world of the reality of Jesus Christ, connect them to His love, and pull in God's end-time harvest of souls.

One of the main reasons for the early church's success was the utilization of all five offices rather than just a few, the way so many of our churches operate today (only the pastor, evangelist, and teacher). For God's end-time Church to bring in the harvest, we must walk in all five anointings. God's "team" must come forth to equip the saints for the work of the ministry. All fivefold ministry gifts are needed to bring the Church to proper balance and order.

Football Is a Team Sport

While at Wake Forest University I was a member of the varsity football team. One thing I learned was that no one person could win the game alone. No matter how good the quarterback is, if he does not have linesmen (guard, tackle, tight end) blocking for him, he will not have time to throw the ball. The quarterback may be the best in the world, but if his defense cannot stop the opposing team from scoring, the quarterback's team will always lose.

Many church leaders have discovered that one man alone cannot do the job. One man cannot bring church into its full function and maturity. Many senior pastors have mistakenly believed they alone can equip the saints under their care. However, God did not design it that way. We need the entire team (pastor, evangelist, teacher, prophet, and apostle) to "win the game." As the Church walks closer to completing its mission (fulfilling the Great Commission), we must allow all the team to play in the game.

Jesus understood the magnitude of the task before Him, and I am certain He understood He could not accomplish His Father's work on His own without the help of others. Seeing the great need of the people and observing that many of His children were desperately lost and had no shepherd, He understood that He needed to draw others into the Father's plan for His life. I believe that in the presence of the Father a plan was devised that would include the recruiting of the 12 young men to assist Him. Realizing the job was too great for just the 12, He later recruited the 70, and this heavenly recruitment has extended even to our times. As we walk into the 21st century, Jesus knows that the harvest in the marketplace is so large that He will need all fivefold ministry gifts in position to equip and train the team. Jesus will need you in position to take your place on the team for this end-time work. God has created each one of us with unique abilities and worked in our lives in such an extraordinary way that it has prepared us in a very special way for the call He has placed upon us. It is critical that we not allow anything or anyone to obstruct the fulfillment of the call.

Divine Relationships

And if one prevail against him, two shall withstand him; and a threefold cord is not quickly broken (Ecclesiastes 4:12).

Living in Chicago, I had the pleasure of watching Michael Jordan play basketball. In an interview, Michael was asked about some of his most memorable basketball experiences. The reporter asked Michael whether the most memorable experience was when he received his sixth championship ring with the Chicago Bulls. Michael paused a second and then answered, "One of my memorable experiences was when I played in the Olympics on the Dream Team representing the United States." On the Dream Team, some of the greatest basketball athletes from America were assembled to represent our great nation.

Likewise, God is bringing His own Dream Team together in the Body of Christ to represent the Kingdom of God. In today's Church, God is recruiting and restoring His Dream Team—His fivefold ministers. We not only have to recognize what God is doing in restoring his fivefold ministers, but protect this new union as well. When Michael Jordan played on the Dream Team, he was recognized as the best player of the world at that time; but he had to realize that the other players were just as important in winning a Gold Medal. Unselfishly, Michael Jordan became a great team player. And because of his team effort, Michael and his teammates did win the Gold Medal for the United States.

God has His own Dream Team and each one of us make up this dynamic line-up of men and women who are committed to the distinct purposes of God for this generation. God has built this team together in such a way that relationships are critical to the effective functioning of this team. By the power of working in union with one another we will be able to fulfill Father's will in these awesome times. Some members of the team might be more visible and have greater responsibility, but even they must understand that they are dependent on those who surround them. There is no member who is irrelevant. All have meaning and purpose and all must be committed to the proper function of the other members.

Teamwork will be a defining feature of God's end-time Church. Each team member will not only know his or her role on the team, but they will also know and respect the roles of the other team members as well. As the Church matures in the Lord, the "one-man" player will fade away. God is raising up team players who can function within a group rather than solely as individuals. The "one-man" team is an archaic concept that must be replaced with God's Dream Team.

If we know in advance that God wants His Body to function together, then we will watch out for the traps of the devil that will prevent us from walking in unity. God's end-time harvest is coming, but to pull in the nets each team member must work in unison with the others.

Now when He had left speaking, He said unto Simon, Launch out into the deep, and let down your nets for a draught. And Simon answering said unto Him, Master, we have toiled all the night, and have taken nothing: nevertheless at Thy word I will let down the net. And when they had this done, they enclosed a great multitude of fishes: and their net brake. And they beckoned unto their partners, which were in the other ship, that they should come and help them. And they came, and filled both the ships, so that they began to sink (Luke 5:4-7).

God is saying to us today, "The catch [of My souls] is too great. I need help! Come help Me pull in My harvest. My nets are breaking." For God's Church to finish the job, each member must be functioning within his or her role to pull in the nets. I need you and you need me. We cannot do the job alone. Let us not only press towards unity within the Body of Christ, but guard carefully the divine relationships that God is putting together.

Humility—A Divine Component

Humility is one of the bonding links that hold the Dream Team together. Humility is not walking around with your head hung down low or saying you are sorry all the time. Humility comes from recognizing the greatness of who God is and the weakness of who we are. One of the key ingredients of humility is "submitting yourself one to another." Humility acknowledges that any gifts and wisdom we have originate with God and not ourselves. We understand that we cannot complete our task without the friendship and support of others. It is our union with Christ and with each other that creates a flow of divine energy that will enable us to accomplish God's will.

God is raising up a Body of believers who will function and act as a team rather than as individuals. Jesus said that the last will be first. Who shall be first in this next Marketplace movement? It is those who serve the people of God walking in God's humility and grace.

If we are going to walk in unity and humility, we must know what each other's duties and functions are within the Body of Christ, so that we can effectively submit to one another. Since the pastor, evangelist, and teacher have been functioning within the Body of Christ for many years, let us look at the roles of the newest kids on the block—the prophet and apostle.

The Role of the Prophet

And are built upon the foundation of the apostles and prophets, Jesus Christ Himself being the chief corner stone (Ephesians 2:20).

Why the prophet? Isn't the prophet found just in the Old Testament? Doesn't the believer have the Holy Spirit now—thus the prophet is not needed anymore in

God's modern-day Church? Can all Christians prophesy? What are the benefits of prophecy? When I was first called to preach in southern Florida, the Lord led me to a prophet in the northern tip of Florida named Bill Hamon, founder of Christian International. Bill was a kind man, but he was different. He was a modern-day prophet. Growing up as a Baptist, I had never heard of such a thing. Later I realized that God had sent me to him to learn more about the role of the prophet in the modern-day Church and why this prophetic gift was important to the Body of Christ.

One day as I was ministering on the beaches in Ft. Lauderdale, the group I was with decided to pray over a homeless man. We all gathered around the man and started to pray one by one over him. When it was my turn, I prayed for his needs, family, and his finding a job. After we had finished praying for him, one lady in the group came over to me and said, "As you prayed, you were prophesying to this brother." In defense, I immediately responded, "I am not prophesying; I am a Baptist." In my denomination, I had never seen someone prophesy or even heard of a prophet, except one found in the Old Testament Bible.

In the defense of Baptists (Methodists, Presbyterians, Lutherans, etc.)—many of them prophesy today, but just don't know it. They have not yet received teaching on the subject. However, we all have the same Holy Spirit. I thank God every day for my Baptist roots and my father, who was a Baptist preacher for 30 years. Whatever church background you may have, I encourage you to discover the benefits of each fivefold ministry office and receive them all into your Christian life.

Desiring Prophecy

From Dr. Bill Hamon's ministry, I discovered that prophecy is for today's Church and that modern-day prophets do exist. Let us now look at three reasons why the Body of Christ should desire prophesying today.

1. *We all need encouragement.*

But one who prophesies, preaching the messages of God, is helping others grow in the Lord, encouraging and comforting them (1 Corinthians 14:4b TLB).

Who does not need encouragement or comfort? Who does not need help to grow in the Lord? I believe that one of the most needed gifts in the Body of Christ is the gift of prophecy. Why? The Body of Christ needs to be encouraged and comforted on a daily basis. One of the biggest misunderstandings that I had in my mind regarding prophecy was that it had to be so "spiritual." God's power would have to "fall upon me" or I had to begin my prophecy with, "Thus says the Lord...." Once again, this mind-set came from my lack of understanding about prophets and the use of prophecy in God's modern-day Church. As I stated earlier, if you are born again, you have the same Holy Spirit. Prophecy is manifested in many ways but one of the simplest manifestations is in divinely given words of encouragement, comfort, or prophetic words that will help you to grow in the Lord. "But one who prophesies speaks to men for edification and exhortation and consolation" (1 Corinthians 14:3 NAS).

2. *We all need to share our faith.*

There cometh a woman of Samaria to draw water: Jesus saith unto her, Give Me to drink....Then saith the woman of Samaria unto Him, How is it that Thou, being a Jew, askest drink of me, which am a woman of Samaria? for the Jews have no dealings with the Samaritans. Jesus answered and said unto her, If thou knewest the gift of God, and who it is that saith to thee, Give Me to drink; thou wouldest have asked of Him, and He would have given thee living water. The woman saith unto Him, Sir, Thou hast nothing to draw with, and the well is deep: from whence then hast Thou that living water? Art Thou greater than our father Jacob, which gave us the well, and drank thereof himself, and his children, and his cattle? Jesus answered and said unto her, Whosoever drinketh of this water shall thirst again: but whosoever drinketh of the water that I shall give him shall never thirst; but the water that I shall give him shall be in him a well of water springing up into everlasting life. The woman saith unto Him, Sir, give me this water, that I thirst not, neither come hither to draw. Jesus saith unto her, Go, call thy husband, and come hither. The woman answered and said, I have no husband. Jesus said unto her, Thou hast well said, I have no husband: for thou hast had five husbands; and he whom thou now hast is not thy husband: in that saidst thou truly. The woman saith unto Him, Sir, I perceive that Thou art a prophet (John 4:7,9-19).

One of the greatest joys in our lives is the opportunity to lead someone to the Lord. I can still remember my first experience as I introduced one of my neighborhood friends to the Lord. One of the methods that Jesus used in the Bible was "felt need" evangelism. It is meeting someone's needs; this event then opens up the heart to receive a greater need through Jesus Christ. For example, one may need a physical healing, something to eat, a place to stay, something to wear, or a miracle from God. Once this individual sees the love of God operating in the life of a Christian who has met this felt need, then the opportunity presents itself to share the gospel. Meeting the felt need first prepares the way for that one to receive the answer to the greater need, which is a relationship with Jesus Christ.

How did the events at the well with the Samaritan woman relate to felt need evangelism and prophecy? First of all, Jesus met the woman's felt needs before He addressed her greater need—eternal life. He met her two needs for respect and acceptance. How did Jesus meet her felt needs? He spoke to the woman and then prophesied to her. Jesus' words to the Samaritan woman at the well were meeting a felt need for respect. In the days of Jesus, Jewish men did not speak to Samaritan women. So the fact that Jesus was talking to her was a big deal in those days. Jesus was giving the Samaritan woman the respect that all human beings deserve and need.

However, Jesus did not stop there. He also met the need for acceptance, never experienced by so many Samaritan women. Jewish men in those days did not talk to women on the street much less non-Jewish women. Jesus was giving her respect and acceptance just by addressing her or talking to her. Every human being desires to be accepted by others and their God. When Jesus prophesied into the Samaritan woman's life (that she had had five husbands and that the man who she was living with now was not her husband), He uncovered the real problem—the woman had problems with receiving acceptance from others. How did Jesus acquire this information about this woman's life? Jesus was prophesying to this woman. This information from Jesus startled the woman and opened her heart to God. She said, "I perceive You are a prophet." Jesus not only met her needs for respect and acceptance, but the way He did it was important as well. By prophesying into her life things that only God could have known, Jesus helped this Samaritan woman to be ready to hear about the more important things of life—her relationship with God.

Every believer has this prophetic capacity. If you want to share your faith and open up the hearts of others to their need for God, prophecy can be a powerful tool.

3. *We all need instruction.*

And He gave some, apostles; and some, prophets; and some, evangelists; and some, pastors and teachers; for the perfecting of the saints [training, equipping] *for the work of the ministry, for the edifying of the body of Christ* (Ephesians 4:11-12).

Many Christians today do not have a proper understanding of the use of prophecy. We usually do not use a gift because we do not understand the gift. Why aren't more Christians encouraging or comforting one another in the Lord through prophecy? Why are not more Christians using the gift of prophecy as a tool to lead others to the Lord? One of the main reasons is the same reason that I did not prophesy—my "lack of understanding." Many in the Body of Christ, for whatever reason, have not been trained in the area of the prophetic. We have been trained to be pastors, because we have accepted pastors. We have been trained as evangelists, because we have accepted the evangelist. We have been trained to be teachers, because we have accepted the teacher. But many of us have not been trained in the prophetic, because we have not accepted the prophet or the gift of prophecy.

We have established the purpose of prophecy within the Church; but what is the purpose of the office of prophet? I believe that one of the primary functions of the prophet is to train the Body of Christ to prophesy. If you have the Holy Spirit within you, then you can prophesy. Many are not using this gift simply because they have not been trained and activated to release it. This is one of the main purposes of the office of the prophet—to train, activate, and release believers to prophesy.

The Role of the Apostle

And are built upon the foundation of the apostles and prophets, Jesus Christ Himself being the chief corner stone (Ephesians 2:20).

In God's end-time Church as we prepare for the harvest coming from the marketplace, we must accept not only the role of the prophet, but also the role of the apostle. Why the apostle? As with prophecy, everyone in the Body of Christ can walk in some dimension of the apostolic anointing. Are all called to the office of the apostle? No! But we all can walk in some dimension of the anointing of the apostle.

As God sent me to Dr. Bill Hamon in Florida to learn more about the importance of prophecy, God also sent me to Chicago to learn more about the role of the apostle in the Church. While in Chicago, God put in my life another anointed man, named John Eckhardt, to increase my understanding. As I read my Bible, prayed, and sat under John's teaching for almost three years, I learned about the various purposes and functions of the office of the apostle. I discovered that the word *apostle* means "a sent one." I learned that God was "sending" the Body of Christ to finish the work of the Great Commission.

To help us further understand the role and function of the apostle, let us look at some of the characteristics of this office.

Signs, wonders, and miracles. (See Second Corinthians 12:12 NIV.) If you are an apostle of a church or a marketplace leader, then the Word you preach should be followed by signs and wonders, e.g. deliverance from evil spirits, healing of the sick, and miracles. This is not the only characteristic of an apostle, but it is the first characteristic mentioned in the Bible with regard to apostles.

Revelation of the calling by an independent witness. (See Acts 13:1-2.) God has a divine order for everything He does. God will establish the "calling" of the apostle by two to three witnesses. This is God's order and way. Do you have a witness?

Ministers are given to apostles. (See Acts 20:4-5.) God gives apostles other ministers to work alongside them. This is called "team" ministry. One of the roles of the apostle is to train and equip the Body of Christ. How do you train and equip if you have no one to be trained? Simply, God gives you people to train. Whether in a church setting or business setting, this kingly anointing is followed with people whom you can train and equip for the Kingdom of God.

Fully functioning churches and businesses. (See First Corinthians 9:2.) Many people can start a church or a business and be successful, but a sign of an apostolic call on one's life is that he can start many churches or many businesses and be successful. I realize that there are "horizontal apostles." Some apostles are "consultants" to many churches and/or businesses rather than having many businesses or churches directly under their authority. Then there are the "vertical apostles" who have a network of churches and/or businesses reporting directly to them, i.e. church planting or business planting. Whether you are a horizontal apostle or vertical apostle, you will be training and equipping other people for the work of ministry. You will have your network, whether as a consultant or overseer. It is critical to note that one of the key signs of an apostle is that an apostle reproduces him/herself.

Serious resistance from evil prince angels. (See Second Corinthians 12:7.) Apostolic ministry may be identified by the amount of opposition it receives. The church in general has misunderstood the apostolic calling. Some think that churches that are not opposed to the apostolic ministry must be blessed and churches that are opposed must not be of God. Quite the contrary is true. Those ministries that lead the way in power and renewal will also find great opposition from the enemy.[3]

Desiring the Apostolic

The office of the apostle is for today's modern Church, and all Christians can walk in a dimension of the apostolic anointing. With that in mind, let us look at three reasons why the Church should accept and receive the anointing of the apostle.

1. *We all need to be "sent."*

The Spirit of the Lord is upon Me, because He hath anointed Me to preach the gospel to the poor; He hath sent Me to heal the brokenhearted, to preach deliverance to the captives, and recovering of sight to the blind, to set at liberty them that are bruised, to preach the acceptable year of the Lord (Luke 4:18-19).

The Body of Christ has been receiving fresh revelation from God for many years now. As we "sit under" the many anointed men and women in the Church today, God is putting a demand on His Church to go to the next level in His purposes. He desires that we finish the job of going to the entire world with the gospel—healing the sick, casting out demons, and preaching a Kingdom message. However, for the Church to be able to finish the job, we must be "sent" by God from the church to the marketplace. Remember, the word *apostle* means a "sent out one." The word *church* means a "called out one." God is calling and sending. The Church must abandon the comfort zone, i.e. the secure confines of the local church, and go out into the workplace, schools, and neighborhoods, compelling others to respond to the love of Christ. He is calling and sending you into this final frontier—the marketplace!

Who will identify, train, empower, activate, and release God's end-time warriors into the final harvest field, the marketplace? Well, you guessed it—the apostle. Yes, all fivefold offices will be used to train the saints, but the office of the apostle is a key foundational office that God needs in place to authorize and release the Body of Christ into its calling.

God is waiting in Heaven for His apostolic leadership to be put in place so He can send out His army into the marketplace. God is waiting for the Church to send trained and equipped saints to the harvest fields. One of the main characteristics of the apostolic dimension is the ability to identify, train, and then send out

Christians to fulfill the callings on their lives. We all need help, a little push, to complete our assignments from God.

> *All power is given unto Me in heaven and in earth. Go ye therefore, and teach all nations, baptizing them in the name of the Father, and of the Son, and of the Holy Ghost* (Matthew 28:18b-19).

Are you ready to go? God is preparing His Church to be sent to do the work of the ministry. God is preparing the Body of Christ to be sent to the marketplace.

2. *We all need to be equipped.*

> *And He gave some, apostles; and some, prophets; and some, evangelists; and some, pastors and teachers; for the perfecting of the saints, for the work of the ministry, for the edifying of the body of Christ* (Ephesians 4:11-12).

The word *perfecting* means "equipping, mending, and training." Many Christians today do not have a proper understanding of the anointing of the apostle. Another function of the apostle is to train and equip you to do the work of the ministry. Many of us have not been trained in the apostolic, because we have not accepted the apostle.

3. *We all need to receive the new emerging apostolic ministry.*

Peter Wagner has had a tremendous influence on my life. Learning to know him and reading the many books he has written, I have discovered that Peter truly has a unique ability to interpret and clearly explain the new moves of God. He is known for his ability to identify the issues regarding church growth. One of his books in particular has really impacted my life. In *Spheres of Authority*, Peter says that not only are apostles a key to the modern-day Church walking in its fullness, but also apostles have different duties and spheres of influence. For example, many church leaders believe for citywide transformation for Christ, but there are reasons why this has not occurred. First of all, many leaders do not know their sphere of influence; secondly, the Body of Christ is still waiting for the marketplace apostles to emerge and take their positions.

A third significant broader sphere of apostolic ministry is marketplace apostles. The vertical and horizontal apostles that I have just described do their ministry primarily in what could be called the nuclear church. Marketplace apostles do their ministry primarily in the extended church. Just as sociologists distinguish between the nuclear family and the extended family, I believe that we can do the same with the church.[4]

For citywide transformation to occur, "congregation apostles" must take their place, mobilizing other apostles, but "marketplace apostles" must be in place as well. If not, the process of citywide transformation will come to a halt. Marketplace apostles are beginning to emerge in the Body of Christ. All apostles must know their calling and sphere of influence, and learn to work effectively with the other members of the "team" in a city…then citywide transformation can occur.

We Need All Fivefold Ministers

As God sends His Church to the marketplace, we are going to need all fivefold ministry offices functioning as a team to finish the job. The pastor, evangelist, teacher, prophet, and apostle are going to have to be accepted, recognized, and functioning within the Body of Christ before the Church will experience the measure of success it desires. Each office is important and each office is necessary to complete the job ahead.[5]

As I have indicated, each believer has a "dual" calling in the marketplace as a king and a priest. Let us now examine the role of a "king" in the marketplace.

Endnotes

1. Ephesians 2:20 NKJV.

2. See John 14:12.

3. John Eckhardt, *Moving Into the Apostolic* (Ventura, California: Renew Books Publishers, 1999), 89-90.

4. Peter Wagner, *Spheres of Authority* (Colorado Springs, Colorado: Wagner Publications, 2002), 78.

5. Marcus Hester, *How to Finish the Job* (Chicago, Illinois: Hester International Publications, 1999), 14.

Section Two

GOD'S WEALTHY CHURCH

...Calling for Marketplace Managers

Chapter 6

THE FINAL FRONTIER

What is the final frontier for the Church? The final frontier is the enormous battle for the souls of men. The heart of a loving God is reaching out through His Church to gather in a harvest of men and women who can be introduced to this loving God. The battle will certainly be intense and the obstacles will be many. One of those obstacles will be the issue of finances. As a people of faith I believe that we will be able to transcend this mighty barrier. The challenge of finances is never a problem with God. He has always found a way to bless and finance that which He initiates. If the Body of Christ is able to spiritually discern the times in which she lives and is willing to lay aside her agenda and commit to the plans and purposes of God then the finances will be supplied. I believe that one of the places where we will see a great harvest of souls is in the marketplace, and from this very marketplace wealth will be extracted in order to fund the vision of God. If we are going to take the gospel to the uttermost parts of the world, then we will need finances to fund the job.[1] Before the Church can complete the assignment, there must be victory in this arena of finances. We must learn how to trust God for the finances we need, and we must prove ourselves worthy of properly handling those finances on His behalf.

Trip to Germany

While in Germany a few years ago on a ministry trip, our team visited the wealthiest cathedral in the world. As I looked at this enormous building with all its gold, the Lord reminded me that it had been dedicated to satan many years ago. In my spirit I heard, "Satan desires to control the financial sector of the world, for if he does, he then controls the other areas as well." From that moment on I started praying with greater intensity, concerning this matter. Later that year, I read a book by Rick Joyner, *Leadership Management and the Five Essentials for Success*. Rick spoke of the "four powers" that control all the earth: the *military, religion, politics,* and *economics*.

> Understanding these four primary sources of power that affect foundational shifts in civilization can provide a paradigm for understanding the general flow of the past, the present, and the future. A paradigm is a model that we use for perceiving, understanding, and interpreting the world. To understand the world today, we must understand that all of the power bases are serving the dominant power base of Economics. This is not a statement of what is right or wrong, but simply what is fact.[2]

Wow! So what Rick is saying is that all four powers are wrapped up in one—economic power.

Rick goes on to say,

> As the world has been moving deeper into the period dominated by the Economic power base, it is clear that most of the world-changing conflicts are Economic in nature. The Cold War was a real war, but an Economic war, not a military war. The great clash between communism and capitalism was an Economic clash more than it was a political clash. The former Soviet Union was beaten Economically, not militarily.[3]

Rick continues,

> Understanding the present nature of this conflict is crucial for any nation that expects to field a successful "army" during this period. The most important "generals" are corporate presidents, bankers, and other economic leaders. The most important army is now composed of workers; small business owners, accountants and other business oriented professionals. Computers are now more important than bombs and bullets. Economics

is now the most powerful force dictating political changes. Economic power base is now more powerful than Military, Religious, or political influences. Economic leadership is the most important kind of leadership that the president must now have."[4]

The final frontier the Church must conquer to fund God's end-time harvest of souls will be this economic frontier. Whoever controls the economic sector will also have power over the religious sector, the political system, and the military. We read in the Book of Revelation that the beast will want to put a mark on all people, even Christians. Why? Satan desires to control all the "buying and selling" of the world. Satan desires to control the world's economy. For satan knows if he can control the economies of the world, he can then control all the other areas of the world systems (religious, political, and military).

And that no man might buy or sell, save he that had the mark, or the name of the beast, or the number of his name (Revelation 13:17).

Prosperity With Purpose

The Church is fighting satan to control the final power of our world—the economic system. However, the Church sees the purpose of money differently than satan does. Greed and power motivate satan. The Church realizes that money is just a tool needed to accomplish an assignment of God. The Church loves God, not money, but must possess this money to finish the task at hand. By understanding this strategy, prosperity takes on a whole new meaning for the believer. I call this newly acquired wealth...*prosperity with purpose* or *money with a mission*. However you look at it, money will be needed. The question remains: Will you have money, or will money have you? God wants to bless His Church, but we must know not only how to obtain finances for the Kingdom, but also how to manage His finances. God owns the world and all its wealth; as Christians we are called to be managers of these financial resources.

How will you respond when God blesses you financially? Will you squander your financial blessings on meaningless and temporal things, or will you allow yourself to be led by the Spirit and discover places where you can invest your money in the Kingdom. Do not misunderstand me. I am not saying that we cannot possess things. We just can't let them possess us. Jesus did not say that money is evil, only the love of money is evil. One of the battlegrounds will be for the wealth of the world! If the Church allows herself to be a funnel of God's blessings, rather than a siphon, is it possible that she might just fulfill her calling to preach the gospel of the Kingdom in all of the earth?

...and the wealth of the sinner is laid up for the just (Proverbs 13:22).

In the next chapter we will explore how God will teach the Church how to obtain and manage that wealth.

Endnotes

1. See Acts 4:32.

2. Rick Joyner, *Leadership Management and the Five Essentials for Success* (Charlotte, North Carolina: Morning Star Publications, 1995), 33.

3. Ibid., 34.

4. Ibid., 35.

Chapter 7

KINGS IN THE KINGDOM

And hath made us kings and priests unto God... (Revelation 1:6).

Before God can finance His end-time harvest, He must set in place financial managers to bring in and manage the finances for the Kingdom of God and to train others with the same purposes! For us to see the God Factor at work in regard to our finances, we have to recognize that God wants to have His appointees established in the marketplace. God wants to place them in positions of influence in order to manage the financial affairs of the world. I refer to these stewards of God's money as *marketplace managers*—they are the ones with the kingly anointing. Another name for this new breed of ministers arising on the Christian scene is *ministers of finance.* These wealth builders will be key "point persons." They will be raised up by God to train and manage others to know how to distribute God's wealth for His end-time harvest of souls.

We will need godly men and women (kings) who are strategically placed in the Body of Christ. They will understand the nature of God's purposes and will be committed to those purposes. These are the ones who will wisely oversee the use of God's money. When I refer to the term *king,* I am referring to both men and women. Every Christian has this "dual" calling of "king and priest" on his life. The kingly anointing is your ability to bring in wealth for the Kingdom of God and to appropriately manage that wealth. Everyone is responsible to learn how to provide for his family, support the church, and effectively manage the balance of these funds.

Jesus Preached a Kingdom Message

And He said unto them, When ye pray, say, Our Father which art in heaven, Hallowed be Thy name. Thy kingdom come. Thy will be done, as in heaven, so in earth (Luke 11:2).

Jesus made the Kingdom message the core of His message, and this involves the training of kings to rule in this kingdom. Like Joseph, who was a steward of Pharaoh's wealth, the Church must faithfully manage these financial resources in order to both fund His future harvest of souls and meet the needs of the poor. The great challenge of the Church today is to issue a call for the "kings" of the Kingdom to be *identified, trained, empowered, and then released* to bring in and manage the wealth of the Kingdom. Will you be the next person who will respond to the kingly call? Can God trust you with this kingly anointing?

In this section we will talk about your kingly call as a *marketplace manager.* Let's look now at the anointing that God is releasing upon His Church—the anointing authority and power to get wealth!

Releasing Power to Get Wealth

But thou shalt remember the Lord thy God: for it is He that giveth thee power to get wealth, that He may establish His covenant which He sware unto thy fathers, as it is this day (Deuteronomy 8:18).

God is releasing upon His Church right now an anointing to get wealth for the Kingdom of God. One of my greatest joys as a minister and businessman is helping people discover their identity in Christ and discover their calling in life. But the other great joy I have as I travel around the world is informing the Body of Christ that we live in a unique time period, where there are numerous opportunities for God's people to gather great wealth for advancing the Kingdom of God.

How will the wealth of the world come to the Church? It will pass through your hands first! God is going to bless you, so you can be a blessing to His Church.

I call this *"prosperity with purpose."* God will bless us in such a way that we can be a part of the fulfillment of His purposes in this generation. The prosperity that we experience has a link to God's purposes on the earth. As a participant in those divine purposes some of you will play a strategic part in the plan. God will pour out a kingly anointing on you to tap into wealth for the purpose of supporting His work in these days. What an awesome blessing, but what an awesome responsibility.

There is much need in the Body of Christ and in the world that cries out for financial support and assistance. It will be your responsibility to carefully consider how that money is spiritually invested in the Kingdom. He is releasing His anointing to bless you so you can then be a blessing to others. Many of you have already experienced that financial prosperity, and I believe that there will be others to follow. As the financial blessings come, then the challenge will be to use those finances in an appropriate way that will further the increase of God's Kingdom. You must be careful of those who will be attracted to you seeking your financial support of their little kingdoms. You will need the wisdom of God so that you can effectively transform these financial blessings into spiritual opportunities for advancing the Kingdom of God. Some people are wondering why their business is growing when the economy is slowing down. Many are perplexed by receiving a job promotion when their coworkers are being laid off. Many are scratching their heads in amazement, wondering how they received a new mortgage for their home, when others are being turned down. God is releasing His grace and favor on the Body of Christ to get wealth for the Kingdom of God. God is releasing His anointing (favor, grace, and power) to get wealth.

At this point I need to mention a couple of crucial factors about getting wealth. First of all, this anointing will not last forever. God always works within time segments. Joseph had seven good years during which to save food, but he knew that Egypt would experience seven years of famine. Right now God is releasing power to get wealth on the Church, but this anointing will not last forever. Many saints come up and ask me, "How long will this anointing last before the 'seven years of famine' begin?" There are many factors to consider, but I believe that you are "in it right now" and you need to walk in the fullness of this anointing. You need to ask for that raise, you need to buy that first house, you need to start the company that has been on your heart, and you need to give to your church like you have never given before. You are under a grace to get wealth.

Secondly, if you do not understand the divine reason for your financial blessings, then during the famine years you will waste all that you have gained. God is blessing you to be a blessing. If you decide to spend your wealth on selfish desires, then God will lift His hand off the financial blessing on your life. Never forget: You are being blessed to be a blessing. You are being blessed to underwrite the harvest of souls that will come from the marketplace. You are being blessed to provide for your family. You are being blessed because God loves you. You are being blessed to bring glory to God. Remember, these "'kingly'" slogans: *prosperity with purpose... money with a mission...wealth mixed with wisdom!*

God's Training and Financial Distribution Centers

And with great power gave the apostles witness of the resurrection of the Lord Jesus: and great grace was upon them all. Neither was there any among them that lacked [great provision]: for as many as were possessors of lands or houses sold them, and brought the prices of the things that were sold, and laid them down at the apostles' feet: and distribution was made unto every man according as he had need (Acts 4:33-35).

In order to receive, manage, and distribute these finances, I believe that we will see the emergence of centers that will help train people in the proper distribution of those finances into strategic geographical areas. A compelling example of a modern-day G.T.F.D.C. is the Dream Center, founded by Tommy Barnett and located in Los Angeles, California. What distinguishes Barnett's church, though, is the staggering array of 200 ministries that operate from the former Queen of Angels Hospital, towering above the Hollywood Freeway. Some of the ministries conduct church services for different ethnic communities, but the vast majority are social service programs targeted at gang members and other at-risk youth, prostitutes,

AIDS patients, the homeless, the hungry, drug addicts—the list goes on. These centers will strategically bridge the gap between the needs of the poor and the resources available from the local government and the church. It will also focus on training new financial leaders who can supervise this wealth for the Kingdom. Yes, many will be trained in resume writing, interviewing, and computer skills in order to open the doors to financial wealth. Others will be trained and released to handle that wealth for the purposes of the Kingdom.

Marketplace managers, whom I call *ministers of finance*, are emerging in the Body of Christ. In this present-day Marketplace movement, it is time the Church recognizes its financial leaders, these *ministers of finance*. They must be strategically positioned in places that will advance God's purposes in these days.

Pastors, many of your future financial leaders are already members of your church waiting for someone to recognize their gifting and calling in the area of finance. You must start recognizing that the role of the Marketplace movement is to get the Church positioned financially to fund God's end-time harvest of souls. Then you must position these newly formed church financial leaders as *marketplace managers* with a kingly anointing.

Dimensions of God's Training and Financial Distribution Centers

"The wealth of the sinner is laid up for the just" (Prov. 13:22b). This means *you*! God is bringing forth a new breed of leader to assist in the restoration of His wealth back into His Church. These *marketplace managers* will need a place to discover, be trained in, and eventually fulfill their "calling." So let us look at some of the characteristics of these training centers that will raise up and send out our future *marketplace managers*.

1. *Training and distribution centers will be places where we can produce leaders of character and wisdom.*

For the love of money is the root of all evil: which while some coveted after, they have erred from the faith, and pierced themselves through with many sorrows (1 Timothy 6:10).

Can you handle money on behalf of the Kingdom? If you receive wealth, will it affect your character? The love of money is the root of all evil. In other words, money is not the problem. The *love of money* is the problem. Money has a way of changing people. It will reveal what has always been in your heart—either good or evil. Money will expose your true character. It is sad to say, but many saints cannot handle money! Why? Money changes them. It exposes lust and desires that will work against the purposes of God. You cannot love both God and money. *Money* is not bad, but the *love* of money is wrong. We are tempted to lose sight of the purposes and plans of God once we receive a little wealth in our pockets. Unfortunately, many believers have to stay "broke, busted, and disgusted" to maintain their walk with the Lord. Money simply changes them. Here is the question you have to ask yourself: Will I remain the same strong Christian whether you have a million dollars or one dollar in my bank account?

The Character Test

If therefore ye have not been faithful in the unrighteous mammon [money], *who will commit to your trust the true riches?* (Luke 16:11)

Many Christians do not understand that they are being "tested" by how they manage their finances. And how they manage their finances is indicative of how they will manage spiritual matters. Whether you know it or not, you are being tested by God every day in how you handle your finances. Many are passing the tests and many are not.

Many people come to me seeking the reason they have not received a "promotion" from the Lord. After asking them just a few questions regarding their personal life and finances, I quickly discover why they have not been promoted yet. When we are in school, to get to the next grade level, we have to pass tests. To move to the next level in our Christian lives, we have to pass a test as well—the character test. Money is the instrument that God uses to test His Church and expose its character.

Character development takes time. As God puts these end-time *marketplace managers* in position of leadership, the chosen ones will be those who have passed the character test in the "pit," even as Joseph passed the text in the pit. If you are going to rule in the palace, you must first pass the "character test" in the pit. Do you want to be one of God's end-time financial leaders (*ministers of finance*)? Then let God develop His character in you. How you pass the character test will determine how God can trust you with His wealth for the Kingdom.

The Wisdom Test

And God gave Solomon wisdom and understanding exceeding much, and largeness of heart, even as the sand that is on the sea shore. And Solomon's wisdom excelled the wisdom of all the children of the east country, and all the wisdom of Egypt (1 Kings 4:29-30).

Not only must you pass the character test, but you must also pass the "wisdom test" to be qualified to handle finances for God's Kingdom. Wealth building requires not only godly character, but also the wisdom of God. We all have a certain degree of earthly wisdom, but godly wisdom is different. Godly wisdom "brings forth the right answer when human wisdom falls short."

Solomon knew he could not perform his job with man's wisdom. He knew he needed God's wisdom. So what did he do? He asked God for more wisdom. In mercy and love, God answered Solomon's prayers. With this newly-possessed wisdom, Solomon became one of the richest men who ever lived on earth. If Solomon needed God's wisdom, how much more do we need it?

How do you get this wisdom from God? Like Solomon, you must ask God.

Ask, and it shall be given you; seek, and ye shall find; knock, and it shall be opened unto you: for every one that asketh receiveth; and he that seeketh findeth; and to him that knocketh it shall be opened (Matthew 7:7-8).

God's wisdom is a gift. You must first pass the "wisdom test." As it takes time to develop character, it also takes time to walk in the wisdom of God. Christians are in a "wisdom test" every day. Have you ever experienced a situation where you said, "How did I get myself into this mess?" Once you solved the problem, you promised yourself that you would be "wiser" next time.

God is watching us to see how we will react to life situations and how we will use God's wisdom to come out victorious. Many times God leads us through "trial and error" situations to develop His wisdom in us. Godly wisdom is acquired through learning from each situation in life in which God places you. As a home is built by placing one brick at a time, so your life is built upon the wisdom of God one situation at a time.

The Body of Christ will need men and women of godly wisdom to manage the huge amounts of finances that will be released to fund the end-time harvest. We cannot keep making the same mistakes over and over. We have to learn from our mistakes, gain new wisdom, and move on to the next level with God. Have you ever made a financial mistake? If you are like me, you have made plenty. However, if I want to be a steward of God's wealth, then I have to stop making those same financial mistakes. In life, each choice (either good or bad) you make will either bring you closer to your goal or take you farther away from it. Failure is not making a mistake, but never trying at all. Another point to add to this axiom is that failure is not making a mistake, but failure is making the same mistake time and time again.

Are you ready to be God's end-time financial leader, a *minister of finance?* Then ask God for wisdom and let God develop His wisdom in you. You must pass both the "character test" and the "wisdom test."

2. *They will be equipping, training, and resource centers.*

And He gave some, apostles; and some, prophets; and some, evangelists; and some, pastors and teachers; for the perfecting of the saints, for the work of the ministry, for the edifying of the body of Christ (Ephesians 4:11-12).

In order to pull in God's end-time harvest of wealth, the Church will need human resources—trained and empowered disciples. Not only will we need trained financial leaders, but we will also need leaders who can train others. One of the main defining features of these centers will be the ability to "reproduce" financial leaders who can be "sent out" to train others in their various churches. These centers will be strong equipping and training centers.

Equipping the Saints of God

As we stated earlier, we are going to need all fivefold ministry offices functioning within the Church to complete the job. As the apostles of finance (ministers of finance) are positioned, one of their main duties will be to train the Body of Christ to handle finances for the Kingdom. These apostolic trainers (*marketplace managers*) will have the wisdom of God to train, equip, and release the saints of God to bring in God's end-time financial harvest.

> *For though ye have ten thousand instructors in Christ, yet have ye not many fathers* [mentors]: *for in Christ Jesus I have begotten you through the gospel* (1 Corinthians 4:15).

In today's Church we have many instructors and preachers, but few fathers. One of the main aspects of the "father spirit" is the father's desire to see his son or daughter become more successful than he was. This selfless quality of the father is needed more than ever in the Body of Christ. Success in your ministry or business is not based on how well you do while you are alive, but on how well the ministry or company functions long after you have passed away. Whom are you reproducing and mentoring to take your place?

Jesus spent the majority of His ministry time training His 12 disciples. He knew that His ultimate success was not based just on what *He* did on earth, but on the effectiveness of the ones He left in charge to carry on the ministry. As a new breed of leaders comes forth in our day, this mentoring fatherly spirit must be the foundation of the equipping process. If this fatherly spirit is not in the hearts of the instructors toward their students, then failure is not far away.

In these centers, many will be trained and equipped to walk in the anointing of the king. For this to happen effectively, we will need to possess the right spirit, the spirit of the Father (Father God).

Resource Centers

These financial centers will make available to the Body of Christ the most recent books, tapes, and videos relating to finances. They will also be places where "pools" of money will be available to fund different Kingdom business opportunities and projects.

For example, one of the greatest needs in the Body of Christ is for many of God's people to purchase a home. Being a homeowner in America has always been a part of the American dream. There are several reasons why someone cannot buy a home: bad credit, not enough monthly income, lack of knowledge about the buying process, or just not enough down payment. As these centers are positioned in the Body of Christ, they can become a resource service that will provide God's people help in buying a home. The center will train prospective buyers to repair bad credit records, evaluate resources, learn about the buying process, and will guide them in applying for financial help for a down payment from the center's real estate fund. From start-up capital for new business projects, to helping people in time of need, these resource centers will have financial resources available for various needs in the Body of Christ and the local community.

They will also supply a list of the various *marketplace managers* who are available to assist you in your various ministries or business needs. From the Marketplace Leaders Speakers Bureau, churches may request a trained marketplace leader to consult with them.

3. *They will be conference and network centers.*

Again, the kingdom of heaven is like unto a net [network], *that was cast into the sea, and gathered of every kind* (Matthew 13:47).

These training and financial centers will be places where key men and women of God with a calling to be "wealth builders" for the Kingdom will meet other men and women of God with similar callings. God is networking the right people together to accomplish His end-time work. The harvest of wealth coming to the Church will necessitate each member of the Body of Christ being in the right position. The Body of Christ must network together as a team.

Marketplace managers will meet other *marketplace managers* through local and regional conferences. These conferences might be the very first time that one will hear of the Marketplace movement. From the "Three-Day Certification" course, to the "National Marketplace Leaders Conference," conducting local, regional, and international meetings has become very important to the spread of the Marketplace movement all around the world.

4. *They will be places to invest into the Kingdom of God.*

Thus saith the Lord, thy Redeemer, the Holy One of Israel; I am the Lord thy God which teacheth thee to profit, which leadeth thee by the way that thou shouldest go (Isaiah 48:17).

Many Christians need help in investing their money. In this Scripture we see that God teaches us how to make a profit with our monies. Why do we fail in our investment opportunities? We simply need godly counsel. The world has produced great investment opportunities, but unfortunately much of the profit goes to fund satan's kingdom rather than God's. We need men and women of God whom we can trust to both make a profit with our money and ensure that those profits will go back into the Kingdom of God. Through our networking efforts at these centers, we will identify godly financial brokers.

Are there other investment opportunities for the Christian? Absolutely! From business ideas…to real estate speculation, God's Training and Financial Distribution Centers will have a team of counselors for your various investments needs.

5. *They will distribute finances to the poor, communities, and needs of the Church.*

If you do not bless the poor, you are missing the "heartbeat" of God. Jesus was always telling His disciples to meet the needs of the poor. These new "kings" who are being raised up will have godly wisdom to know how to distribute God's funds to the poor.

And the saying pleased the whole multitude: and they chose Stephen, a man full of faith and of the Holy Ghost (Acts 6:5a).

Modern-day Stephens, men and women full of the Holy Spirit and faith, are coming forth to care for the poor. The centers will oversee distributions to the poor as well as to other community and church needs. As God positioned Joseph to administrate the distribution of wheat during the seven years of famine, He will also set in place modern-day Josephs whom He can trust to meet the needs of His Church and the surrounding communities. These new "kings" will be full of godly wisdom to distribute great amounts of wealth.

6. *They will be places where new ideas and new technologies for the Church will be released.*

The world we live in is ever changing. New inventions and new technologies greet the consumer almost every day. This new technology is vital to the Christian's success in business or ministry. With the invention of the Internet, our way of communication has changed forever. The Internet offers limitless opportunities; the Body of Christ will be wise to maximize these resources.

God's Training and Financial Distribution Centers will produce *marketplace managers* with character and wisdom. They will be places to equip and train finance ministers. These centers will be conference and network centers that provide opportunities to invest in the Kingdom of God. From the base of these centers they will distribute finances to communities and churches. They will inform Christians of the most recent inventions, technologies, and ideas to enhance business or ministry efforts.

Wealth Builders (God's Kings)

The Body of Christ is about to experience one of the greatest harvest of souls from the marketplace that the Church has ever seen. In order to fund the harvest,

God is releasing kings into His Kingdom with *great power, great grace,* and *great provision (wealth)* to finish the job. These kings *(marketplace managers)* will not only bring in the financial harvest, but will train others in managing finances through God's Training and Financial Distribution Centers.

God is releasing "kings" for His Kingdom—the God Factor. Who will heed the call to the marketplace to be God's kings? Who will respond to God's timetable in these days?

Chapter 8

WALKING IN GOD'S TIMETABLE

To every thing there is a season, and a time to every purpose under the heaven (Ecclesiastes 3:1).

Timing is key to all activities in the marketplace. For example, to make a profit in the stock market, I have to buy low and sell high. If I miss the timetable of when to buy or when to sell, I could lose all my money. In the same way, our success in walking with God is determined by our ability to walk in God's timing. In God's Kingdom, there is a season for everything. The Greek word *kairos* means "a season, a time, or a period."[1] As Christians, we often fail to see God's timing in the circumstances in our lives.

The Window of Opportunity

Why is timing important to God's end-time harvest of wealth and His harvest of souls? Simply, God's "outpouring" of His blessing will not last forever. There are seasons of His blessing. Our job as Christians is to synchronize our lives with His timing and to harmonize with His purposes in the world.

As an "ambassador" for the Marketplace movement, I sometimes speak to crowds who have never heard of it. One of the first subject matters I address is the *kairos* timing of God. Why? If people do not understand how God is moving right now within the Body of Christ (individually and corporately), then the message of the Marketplace movement will be lost.

But thou shalt remember the Lord thy God: for it is He that giveth thee power to get wealth [right now anointing], *that He may establish His covenant which He sware unto thy fathers, as it is this day* (Deuteronomy 8:18).

Although we can't presume that God might or might not be blessing His Church five or ten years from now, we do know that right now He is pouring out His Spirit on His people.

One of the critical factors in making a real estate purchase is location, location, location. In a similar fashion, in the Kingdom of God, success depends on timing, timing, timing! If we are entering into a time of unusual financial blessing, then it will be essential to recognize this divine opportunity and fully cooperate with God's purposes. To further understand the principal of God's timetable, we will look at the life of Joseph.

The Joseph Company

Behold, there come seven years of great plenty throughout all the land of Egypt: and there shall arise after them seven years of famine; and all the plenty shall be forgotten in the land of Egypt; and the famine shall consume the land (Genesis 41:29-30).

The story of Joseph is an interesting one. We all know that his brothers sold him into slavery, but he eventually became the ruler of all Egypt under Pharaoh. Joseph was the boy who went from the "pit to the palace," the boy who could interpret dreams. He seemed to have been forgotten, but eventually God positioned him to save his whole family (nation of Israel).

Just as God used Joseph of old, He is positioning His Church to save not only the Church, but also the whole world. God always has a plan. Thinking ahead of us, God is always preparing a future timetable.

In interpreting Pharaoh's dream, Joseph told the ruler that he had seven good years to get ready for the seven years of famine that would follow. I believe God's Church is in a season of great economic blessing. It is not predicated on what the stock market does or what the unemployment numbers are. Simply, right now God is pouring out His financial blessing on the Church in preparation for His end-time harvest of souls.

A Time to Build

And the Lord said unto Noah, Come thou and all thy house into the ark; for thee have I seen righteous before Me in this generation. Of every clean beast thou shalt take to thee by sevens, the male and his female: and of beasts that are not clean by two, the male and his female. Of fowls also of the air by sevens, the male and the female; to keep seed alive upon the face of all the earth. For yet seven days, and I will cause it to rain upon the earth forty days and forty nights; and every living substance that I have made will I destroy from off the face of the earth. And Noah did according unto all that the Lord commanded him (Genesis 7:1-5).

God's timing of spiritual blessing is important; it is also important to know how to use this blessing in preparation for the future harvest. Noah knew that there was a time to build, but there would later be a time to get in the boat. The Church is in a "building" season or "preparation" season now. Right now God is pouring out His Spirit on our finances so we can get the Church in position to handle the new converts who will enter His Church. Noah spent 120 years building a boat for a period of rain that would last 40 days. Jesus spent 30 years preparing for a period in His life that would last only three and one-half years. The maiden Esther prepared one year to spend only one night with the king. We too are in a season of preparation, but we must use our time, energy, and finances properly. The preparation might be long and arduous, and the time of blessing might be short. This is why we must prophetically understand the times in which we live.

Seven Years of Plenty or Seven Years of Famine

Like Joseph we must be prophetically sensitive and practically astute so that we can maximize every financial blessing that comes our way. The finances that are channeled into the Kingdom of God must be clearly earmarked for their divinely intended direction. We never know what might happen during these turbulent times. What we must do is take advantage of what God has graced us with and use that for the ongoing thrust of the Kingdom of God into the world cultures. We must be wise as Joseph and carefully calculate, through prayer, every move we make. We certainly should avoid the old and ineffective paradigms and be willing to step out in faith, if God asks us to do things we never imagined.

I conclude this chapter with *eight steps* that I believe will help you get the most out of the times in which we live:

1. Realize that there are some of you in a season of financial blessing. Acknowledge it (to yourself and family) and to God. Simply say "yes" to God!

2. Recognize that your past financial mistakes, attitudes, and actions can hinder your future financial success. Ask the Lord to reveal any past financial mistakes and repent of them. This creates a clean (financial) slate in your life from which the Lord can now work. I call this action step "positioned for blessing."

3. Realize that prosperity with purpose means that you are being blessed to be a blessing to others and to the cause of Christ. Commit in your heart that it is "better to give than receive."

4. Grasp the fact that this season of blessing presents opportunities that otherwise would not have been available. You are in an "open heavens" situation. Be willing to step out in faith in your job, new business opportunities, etc. The favor of the Lord is upon you.

5. Remember that your success is based on receiving wise counsel. Seek others who can help you in your business decisions. Find godly friends who can support you and stand with you in prayer as you seek to wisely invest your financial blessings.

6. Understand that the door can only be opened if you knock. Keep on knocking, seeking, and finding. Your determination and persistence are keys to reaching your goal.

7. Accept the truth that prayer will pave the way. In this new Marketplace movement, prophetic prayer will move you faster to your destiny. Prayers

of agreement and supplication will be mixed with prayers of declaration and decree.

8. Understand that "hearing the voice" of God will be important to reaching your goals and obeying the voice of God will be a priority.

God is establishing "kings" in His Kingdom to bring in the end-time financial harvest to fund His end-time harvest of souls. Right now there are many in the Body of Christ who are or will be entering into a "season" of financial blessings. Each believer has a "dual calling." You are not just a king in the marketplace, but you are a priest as well. Let us now look at your "priestly call" as a marketplace leader—the God Factor.

Endnote

1. From *Vine's Expository Dictionary of Biblical Words* (Nashville, Tennessee: Thomas Nelson Publishers, 1985).

Section Three

GOD'S MINISTERING CHURCH

...Calling for Marketplace Ministers

Chapter 9

GOD IS "EXPANDING" HIS ANOINTING

And hath made us kings [marketplace managers] *and priests* [marketplace ministers] *unto God and His Father; to Him be glory and dominion for ever and ever. Amen* (Revelation 1:6).

As the role of the king is changing, the role of the priest (*marketplace ministers*) is changing as well. Many church leaders (fivefold ministers) today have missed their true calling. The Body of Christ has missed its true calling as well. In the present-day Marketplace movement, God is about to change the way we do church. He is about to reveal another God Factor that will give you the edge at work and change forever the way you perceive your work. You can find work to be a joy rather than a burden.

The Role of the Fivefold Ministry

And He gave some, apostles; and some, prophets; and some, evangelists; and some, pastors and teachers [fivefold ministers]; *for the perfecting of the saints, for the work of the ministry, for the edifying of the body of Christ* (Ephesians 4:11-12).

As believers, we have to go back to the original purpose of the fivefold ministry gifts, which was to perfect—that is equip and train—the Body of Christ to do God's work. Unfortunately, pastors have performed their pastoral responsibilities, but have not taught the Church to be pastors. Teachers have taught others, but have not taught their students to be teachers themselves. Evangelists have won others to Christ, but have not taught the Body of Christ to be soul winners. Prophets have given inspirational words to the Church, but have not taught the Church to prophesy. And apostles have been sent out to establish new works, but have not taught others so they can be sent out to do the work of the ministry. Many spiritual leaders today have created a codependent relationship on their ministry rather than on God. Many local churches have become "entertainment" centers where the members come together each Sunday and watch the worship team and the pastor perform, rather than becoming training centers where the people are asked to perform—that is, to actually do the work of the ministry. Whose fault is it? The spiritual leaders are partly to blame, but the Body of Christ is partly to blame as well.

> *And He shall turn the heart of the fathers to the children, and the heart of the children to their fathers, lest I come and smite the earth with a curse* (Malachi 4:6).

In the last days, Malachi the prophet said, God is going to turn the hearts of the fathers to the children and the children to the fathers. However, this plan will not work unless fathers learn how to be fathers and start functioning like fathers; and children start functioning like children. In other words, the Body of Christ and the fivefold ministers must start walking in their design assignments from God. In this new pattern, ministers and spiritual leaders will begin to operate as spiritual equippers, training Christians to do the work of the ministry.

In the Marketplace movement, the fivefold spiritual leaders will regain their positions as equippers and trainers. It is my prayer that many spiritual leaders will become convicted of not walking in their true calling, repent before their congregations, and start to move in a new direction.

I have seen this happening all over the world. In many pastors' gatherings, we are observing full altars, as spiritual leaders repent of not walking in the "fullness" of their callings as equippers to the Body of Christ.

The Church is in a paradigm shift. God is moving through His fivefold spiritual leaders to reclaim their rightful places within the Body of Christ. These leaders will be strategic in the preparation and mentoring of the Body of Christ for the great work that is before us. This is the time to break the old paradigms of ministry. Leaders were never meant to exclusively "do the work." They are called for the purpose of training and equipping the saints so that they do the work as *marketplace ministers.*

Taking the "Baby Bottle" Away

As a father of three children, I watched my children grow up. Each stage of life presents different challenges (infancy, toddler, child, teenager, and young adult). One challenge that all mothers and fathers face is taking the baby bottle away from the toddler. While the parent knows that the child needs solid food to move to the next stage of life, the child does not know that something better awaits him. He only knows that the bottle is pretty good and thinks that nothing could ever replace it.

As the parent, you know that if you do not take the bottle away, the toddler will never experience the joy of eating chicken, mashed potatoes, nice hot rolls coming from the oven, and hot apple pie. The child needs not only the experience of eating solid food, but also the nutrition supplied by these foods, which will help the child grow up to be big and strong. Who does not want this kind of growth for their child?

Likewise, Father God in His mercy and love wants each one of us to be all we can be in Christ. He desires for us to fulfill our calling on this earth. He wants us to grow up in the Lord and begin to discover His plan and purpose for our life. What is holding the Body of Christ back from being all it can be in Christ? We are still holding onto our spiritual "baby bottles." Many believers today are sitting in church every Sunday morning waiting for the pastor to deliver another inspiring sermon. We enjoy our churches and our pastors and (heaven forbid) please do not ask us to do anything for the Lord. This attitude in the Body of Christ *has to change.*

They All Had Baby Bottles in Their Mouths!

Many years ago, I was preaching to a large audience one Sunday morning on the subject of being "a priest in the workplace." It was like any other Sunday morning, but as I began to minister, the Lord flashed a vision in front of my eyes. In the vision, I saw every member of the congregation clothed in baby clothes, with baby bottles in their mouths. This vision startled me but quickly disappeared. When I finished that sermon, all I wanted to do was get alone to pray.

Back in my hotel room, I got on my knees and asked the Lord, "Why were all the people in the church clothed in baby clothes and sucking on baby bottles?" I did not wait long for an answer. The Lord spoke to my heart, "To Me, this is what many churches look like, as I gaze from Heaven. Many of My saints have never grown up to experience what it means to be mature Christians. They are still looking to be spoon-fed rather than to feed others. They have refused to grow up." I responded, "Lord, who will take the baby bottles away so each believer can experience the greater things of the Kingdom?" He answered, "I have called you to be an instrument in My hand to take the bottles away and teach My children how they must give up childish things."

Without a doubt, there are many in the Body of Christ who have realized that they also are called into the work of the Lord. They have discovered that they have unique gifts and a special calling in what God is doing in this time. They have abandoned the old ways and have arisen to take up the challenge. I am not addressing these saints.

I am addressing those who still live in the old ways and either do not understand their gifting and calling or have refused to respond to the challenge of these days. They are quite content to sit in church and allow the pastor to spiritually feed them and let him do what they should be doing. For these ones it is time to take the bottle out of their mouth.

As the Lord spoke to me, I remembered how our children responded when my wife and I began the process of weaning them. I remembered the sleepless nights and the crying (and screaming). I did not like those times in our children's lives. But then I remembered that our children *did* make it through that period of life. I asked the Lord one more question. "How can one ever begin to do such a job of weaning the Body of Christ off its spiritual bottles? This is an impossible job!"

The Lord spoke to my heart one more time, "I have already begun the weaning process. You will see many changes to My Church in the years ahead. You will hear of screaming, crying and protesting from the Body, but trust Me and know that all I am doing is for good and not bad. I will need My whole Body in position for the next work I want to do in My Church. As I complete the weaning process I will release great grace upon My Church."

Why Is the "Baby Bottle" So Difficult to Part With?

As the Church moves away from its comfort zone, God's people will walk into a new dimension. The believer (not just the fivefold ministry team) is going to be the "minister" doing the work of the Lord. The church leader will be the equipper. The saint will be the harvester. For the Church to walk into its next level, we are going to have to walk outside our comfort zones and start taking risk for the Kingdom.

God's Church is about to grow up. There are many other ways to drink and eat, but more importantly, the Church must be weaned from its appetite for baby food. In this next Marketplace movement, the ambassadors for the movement will preach many messages that will stress the benefits of giving up the bottle. Most of us are seldom willing to give up something unless we first have something to replace it. Once the Body gets a revelation that "greater works" and "great blessings" lie around the corner for those who are mature, then giving up our spiritual "baby bottles" will be much easier.

In this process we must deal with fear. Human nature likes a safe environment rather than change. These end-time everyday saints will be the ministers of the workplace. They will be meeting new people. They will have to overcome the fear of sharing their faith. They will have to deal with the fear of losing their jobs if they are faithful to their calling.

> *Behold, I send you forth as sheep in the midst of wolves* [overcoming fear]*: be*
> *ye therefore wise as serpents, and harmless as doves* (Matthew 10:16).

End-time priests (*marketplace ministers*) will have to overcome fear to walk in the fullness of their calling into the marketplace (workplace, schools, neighborhoods, etc.)

We must also deal with the power of religion. In Jesus' days, religion was a major obstacle to spreading the gospel. Today, the Church is facing similar obstacles. Unfortunately, many churches today are more interested in experiencing God for themselves than in sharing that experience with someone else. During the past "revival movement," many saints became addicted to a "feeling" they experienced in those meetings. They have never come to the place of understanding the *purpose* of being revived. During the "revival movement" God was attempting to get His Church in a revived position, so He could then move forward to bring true revival in the marketplace. In this next Marketplace movement, we must confront and overcome the spirit of religion.

One of the Church's Greatest Challenges

During the late 1990s, in the Apostolic movement, God was "shifting" His leadership in the Church. Many pastors had apostolic callings on their lives, but they did not know how to make the transition. John Eckhardt's book, *Leadershift: Transitioning From the Pastoral to the Apostolic* helps leaders in this transition period.

Eckhardt writes, "Because of this restoration of the ministry of apostle, we must redefine the role and function of the pastor. With restoration comes reformation. This will be painful for many who resist change and cannot see any other way of doing ministry."[1] However, the transition to the Marketplace movement need not be painful—if we just line up with what God is doing in this day and hour.

As God is shifting His anointing now to extend from the fivefold leadership team to the whole Body of Christ (the Saints), the role of the saint is about to change. Many churches today have only addressed the "felt needs" of the Body of Christ, but have never challenged and equipped the believers to discover and walk in their true calling as *marketplace ministers.*

The Anointing Is Available to All

And Stephen, full of faith and power, did great wonders and miracles among the people (Acts 6:8).

Not only will the fivefold ministers assume their role as equippers of the saints, but the Body of Christ (everyday believers) must realize that God has expanded His anointing to the whole Body of Christ. *Every* Christian will have a part to play in this movement into the marketplace. No one will be left out!

In Acts 6:8, Stephen, probably a businessman, was one of the first deacons of his church. Along with the other deacons he was enlisted to buy some bread for the widows of the church. With great wisdom the deacons supervised this distribution to the Jewish and Gentile women who were fighting with each other. I think that in fulfilling his task he discovered that "wonders and miracles" would follow him. In the marketplace, Stephen performed miracles like the original 12 apostles had done. Two major events occurred here with Stephen, and the same two events are occurring today with the Marketplace movement.

Many are discovering that the anointing is not just for a selected few. It is for the whole Body of Christ. The anointing that was on the 12 apostles had come to rest upon Stephen, and that same anointing is available to every child of God. Stephen was not a theologian or priest, nor did he attend a Jewish seminary. Stephen was somebody just like you and me. However, on that day that Stephen went to the marketplace his life changed forever.

As we enter into the marketplace, God is making it clear that He has equipped us with His power and given us great wisdom to fulfill His purposes in every place where people gather. In order to accomplish this, *God is making us understand that the anointing for business and for serving God in the workplace has always been available to us.* He is not taking away His anointing from His fivefold ministers; He is just causing us to see that His anointing is not limited only for leaders. He is releasing an anointing on His whole Body to fulfill their call and to impact the culture around them. He is releasing a grace and anointing for all to be ministers in the marketplace. This is your priestly call. God desires to anoint you for your specific placement in this world.

But the anointing which ye have received of Him abideth in you (1 John 2:27a).

I believe that in these days God is releasing and expanding a new measure of His grace and power to the Body of Christ in order that they might bring in the harvest.

How is God going to do this? He is pouring out His Spirit upon all flesh so that they might be anointed ministers in their places of employment. As we become ambassadors for God in our workplaces, schools, neighborhoods, and local supermarkets, then "wonders and miracles" will begin to follow us as well.

Not only is God expanding His anointing upon His entire Church, He is also performing miracles in new locations. In the early church, the majority of miracles, healings, deliverances and "signs and wonders" performed by the apostles did not occur in the local church but within the marketplace (39 of the 40 miracles recorded in the New Testament).

I think the early apostles knew something that many of us in the Body of Christ have not recognized yet. Could it be that our success in ministry is based not only on being anointed, but also by where we minister? Stephen's ministry success was determined by God's anointing for wonders and miracles, *and* by where he performed these miracles—the marketplace!

The Marketplace Call

Now when He had left speaking, He said unto Simon, Launch out into the deep, and let down your nets for a draught. And Simon answering said unto

Him, Master, we have toiled all the night, and have taken nothing: nevertheless at Thy word I will let down the net. And when they had this done, they enclosed a great multitude of fishes: and their net brake. And they beckoned unto their partners, which were in the other ship, that they should come and help them. And they came, and filled both the ships, so that they began to sink (Luke 5:4-7).

God is calling out to His Church, "I need help bringing in the final harvest of souls from the marketplace. Everyone get in position (your corner of the net) so not one fish will be lost (to eternal damnation)." The Church is being weaned off the "bottle" and is about to grow up. Regardless of who you are—a housewife, a student, an athlete, a political figure, a janitor, an insurance salesman, a postal worker, or CEO of your company—God is calling all those who will say "yes" to Him. Will you say "yes" to God? Are you the next one who will do great things for God at your workplace?…in your classroom?…in your neighborhood? *He is not looking for your ability; He is just looking for your availability!* I challenge you today to simply say, "yes"…to Him!

Let's now explore how you can get prepared (trained, empowered, and released) to walk into the fullness of your priestly call.

Endnote

1. John Eckhardt, *Leadershift: Transitioning From the Pastoral to the Apostolic* (Chicago, Illinois: Crusaders Ministries, 2000), 7-8.

Chapter 10

PRIEST IN THE PARLIAMENT

Go ye therefore [the saints…to every fiber of our society and culture], *and teach all nations, baptizing them in the name of the Father, and of the Son, and of the Holy Ghost* (Matthew 28:19).

In America we have a saying: "You can ask me about anything…but do not ask me about my political views or religious beliefs." Many unchurched folks would love to believe that the forefathers of this great nation made it law that there was to be a "separation of the church (God) and the state (local government)." However, our founding fathers never intended it so. Our government should not impose on us what we should believe, but as Christians living in a free society we should have the right to express our religious beliefs and opinions in the public arena, including our schools and workplaces. The Parliament is Britain's national legislative body, similar to our Congress, and they are responsible for governing the whole nation. As we walk into this new move in the marketplace, God is about to take His rightful seat back in "Parliament." He is about to take His rightful seat back in our government offices, school boards, and corporate boardrooms, where decisions are made that will affect our nation. Man is trying to "kick God out" of our schools, governments, and public venues…but let me make a statement loud and clear: *God is coming back, and He is coming back with a bang!*

He is coming back by sending you (His priest) to represent Him. Many of you will be running for political office to bring God back into government. You will be seated on the next school board making decisions that will bring glory to God. Many of you will be at the next corporate board meeting, voting against a decision that is not following the principles of God. It is clear that God is mobilizing His ambassadors to enter into the marketplaces of the world!

You Are the Church

For where two or three are gathered together in My name, there am I in the midst of them (Matthew 18:20).

We have been talking about how God is shifting His focus from the four walls of the church. He is simulating the life of the church in the marketplace. The actual Church is not a building or a place; it is a people. *You are the Church!* If you are a born-again Christian, then you are the Church. Wherever you go, there goes the Church. A Christian friend asked me if our church was growing. Having just finished a Thanksgiving meal, I looked down at my stomach and said, "Yes, it seems that it is!" We laughed at that statement, realizing that church growth really is not in the size of a person's physical body—but the truth is that you are the Church. So wherever you go—neighborhood, school, workplace, and supermarket—*there goes the Church*. Most of the world will never enter inside the borders of a church building. However, when the saints realize that they are the Church, they will take the Church to the people, rather than wait for people to come to church. The sinner in the world encounters the Church every day (you in the marketplace), but the problem remains that many saints still associate the word *church* with the building where they meet on Sunday mornings.

Have you ever considered this? You might be the only Jesus that those around you will ever meet. For us to fulfill our calling in the marketplace, God has to make some adjustments in our thinking! We have to redefine *what* the Church is, *where* the Church is, and *who* the Church is. It is not a group, organization, denomination, or building. *You* are the Church—the Bride of Christ!

Many of us have heard of the church planting (missionary) efforts of many church leaders around the world. They share with us how they are planting churches all over the world in record numbers. New buildings are being put in place, and people from all over the surrounding rural areas are coming together to meet on

Sundays. All this is good, but there is a new wave of church planting that will occur in the new Marketplace movement. I see God doing a new thing. Instead of traditional churches being established that focus on the Sunday meetings, I see new churches being established in workplaces, schools, and neighborhoods. Jesus said, "If two or three are gathered together in My name, there I am in the midst of you." In other words, when "two or three of you" gather together on your lunch hour to pray for your company, then *you are having church*! When "two or three" of you decide to pray for your school during your recess period, then *you are having church*! When a mother with three kids asks a neighbor over during her free time to pray for her neighborhood, then *you are having church*! Should you remain a member of a local church? Absolutely! However, church is not limited to a building or a place. As God's people leave the perimeters of the church building, so goes the Church, taking the message of the Kingdom into the marketplace!

Is the Church Losing the Battle?

Because my dad, Dr. Joe Hester, was a pastor for over 30 years, I witnessed firsthand the internal structure and dynamics of many churches. I have seen a lot of successful ministry as well as a lot of unsuccessful ministry. I have seen saints mature in the Lord in a church, and I have seen saints leave churches with hurting and bitter hearts. I have observed pastors as they pioneer new works and I have seen pastors take over the work of another man. I have seen pastors with large church staffs and I have witnessed pastors with a staff of one person—themselves. However, one thing I have realized, and I am sure you will agree: The Church has a long way to go—and in many areas it is simply losing ground—before we finish the work of the Great Commission.

Approximately one third of the world has professed Christianity, one third of the world is Hindu, and another one third of the world is Muslim. In many countries, the Muslim and Hindu faiths are doubling in size every year. However, in many places, conversions to Christianity have slowed to zero in a given year. In some communities, the church doors are closing down. I know this is not accurate for all Christian communities, but there seems to be something awfully wrong with our archaic methods of reaching the world. It seems to me that God has a better way of doing church.

God Is Frustrating Our Plans

I do believe God allows us to fail at times. Why? It is apparent to me that our future success is indicative of our present failures. Let me explain what I mean. Sometimes, God has to frustrate our plans and methods, so we will humble ourselves and get desperate enough to abandon our ways and seek *His* will and way for our circumstances. Your failure might be the greatest thing that has ever happened to you.

In my book, *How to Finish the Job*, I describe how God is releasing a "holy frustration" on the Body of Christ. This "holy frustration" has caused many believers to experience revival and to find the perfect will of God for their lives.[1]

Recently, I was talking with a pastor friend, and he asked me, "Marcus, why hasn't my church grown over the last several years? In fact, it is smaller than it has ever been." Before I gave him an answer, I told him I would seek the Lord regarding this and get back to him. In my prayer time, I asked the Lord, "Lord, why is it that my friend's church is not growing?" The Lord spoke to my heart, "He was not called to be a pastor. He was called to be a businessman for the Kingdom. If he walks in his grace, things will start to turn around for him."

This was not what I wanted to hear. How could I tell my friend that he needs to give up his pastoral position and become a businessman? Well, I obeyed God and told Jim. For many months, he rejected the notion that he was to give up the pastorate. One day, with tears of holy frustration, he came to tell me he would obey the Lord. How is Jim doing today? Well, Jim is now one of the most successful businessmen of his city. He is traveling around the world speaking to other businessmen for Christ. Jim's life is being blessed! God frustrated his plans, so that Jim could find the divine assignment for his life. Jim found his "grace zone," but he had to first lay *his* ideas and ways at the cross of Jesus.

Is God frustrating your plans? It might not be the devil that is causing all your problems, but God. God just might be giving you a big dose of "holy frustration."

Then comes the question...how do we respond to God when we feel that our plans are being frustrated? I will give you the short answer. Humble yourself, listen to the voice of the Lord, seek the mind of God regarding your situation, and then obey Him when He reveals the answer.

*And it shall come to pass, if thou **shalt hearken diligently** unto the voice of the Lord thy God, to observe and to **do all His commandments** which I command thee this day, that the Lord thy God will set thee on high above all nations of the earth* (Deuteronomy 28:1, emphasis added).

Many Christians today are frustrated with the state of the Church. Many Christians want to do more for God. Could it be that God is frustrating our plans? Could it be that God has a better and more efficient way of doing church—the God Factor? God is showing His Church a new way to reach the world with the gospel. Are you frustrated with the progress of the Church? Then you are right where you need to be, because in the Saints movement (Marketplace movement), God is releasing on the Body of Christ a "holy frustration" that is causing many believers to get on their knees and seek God for His answers and His better ways.

The Father's Heart

And He shall turn the heart of the fathers to the children, and the heart of the children to their fathers, lest I come and smite the earth with a curse (Malachi 4:6).

One of the greatest motivating forces for changing the present course of this world is *love*. It was the constant theme of our Lord. It was the passion of the early church, and if we are to have any significant impact on our culture, the love of God must be rediscovered and demonstrated by the whole Body of Christ. For this to happen we must understand the nature of our heavenly Father.

Many believers today have never experienced the blessing that comes from the "fatherly" ministry of the fivefold ministry gifts; rather the ones they have been exposed to are operating out of "control" rather than the Father's love. This controlling spirit that characterizes too many leaders, is founded in a tragic sense of insecurity and must be broken if those leaders are going to become significant in these days. We are not called to control others but to release them into their callings. A controlling spirit will only hinder what God is doing in this day.

In the Marketplace movement, God's end-time ministers must operate in the love of the Father. *Marketplace ministers* will walk humbly before one another with the spirit of a servant. Pride will not be able to raise its ugly head in this new movement. The saints will be motivated to join in, because they will feel the love of the Father coming through the hearts of the leaders, helping them to be all they can be in Christ.

People will want to serve leaders who care for their welfare and have the Father's love flowing from their hearts. God's end-time leaders, who will train God's *marketplace ministers*, must and will operate in the spirit of the Father's love.

I think it is interesting to note that this Scripture in Malachi is the last verse found in the Old Testament. As we are walking in an end-time move with the Marketplace movement, it is critical to understand and accept the "Father's heart" anointing. It is this anointing that will help us to finish the task at hand. People will never be motivated by a dictatorial style of leadership. People are motivated by the love and passion of leaders who genuinely care for their well-being and want to support their calling in life.

Many times a person's success is not based just on what they do, but on how they do it. A leader's attitude and motivations in performing a thing are just as important as the actual performance of the task.

The Greatest Call in the World

And Jesus, when He was baptized, went up straightway out of the water: and, lo, the heavens were opened unto Him, and He saw the Spirit of God descending like a dove, and lighting upon Him: and lo a voice from heaven, saying, This is My beloved Son, in whom I am well pleased (Matthew 3:16-17).

The greatest calling in Heaven or earth is to be a saint of the Most High God. There is no greater privilege or position than that of being His son or daughter. I do not care what title you may have (apostle, prophet, pastor, evangelist, teacher, Sunday school teacher, nursery worker, etc.), the playing field is all equalized at the cross.

In the Body of Christ, it appears that we are more interested in titles and positions than simply and faithfully fulfilling the task to which we are called. Titles and positions are fine in helping us identify our roles within the Body of Christ, but when we use them to elevate ourselves in pride, then we have misunderstood the purpose of our role. When John baptized Jesus, God did not look down upon His Son and say, "This is My beloved apostle or pastor, in whom I am well pleased." No! God addressed Jesus as His "Son"! We are all saints of the Most High. Yes, we will all be judged by how we accomplished our life assignment here on this earth, but our main goal is to yield to God as He transforms us to the likeness of His Son—Jesus!

For whom He did foreknow, He also did predestinate to be conformed to the image of His Son, that He might be the firstborn among many brethren (Romans 8:29).

Yes, God has given a tremendous assignment to His Church in fulfilling the Great Commission. That is the task He has given us, but let us keep before us what our even greater purpose is—to let God transform us into the image of His Son Jesus. Is there an honor in being "just a son or daughter" of God? You bet there is! You are already walking in the greatest calling you will ever have—the calling to be a saint of the Most High God. Don't worry about titles or ministry functions in the Church, but celebrate just being a saint. You are a son or daughter of the Most High God. Nothing can be greater than that! Titles can become a snare that will "puff us up." We are called to a love that will build us up and mold us into the image of His Son.

Motivating and Releasing the Saints

As we approach the fullness and final stages of the Saints movement, I believe that there are three major events that will occur:

- Saints will receive new revelation.

- Saints will be equipped.

- Saints will be released.

1. *Saints will receive new revelation.*

The king answered unto Daniel, and said, Of a truth it is, that your God is a God of gods, and a Lord of kings, and a revealer of secrets, seeing thou couldest reveal this secret (Daniel 2:47).

When God begins to move in new directions in His created world, He will always have a mouthpiece on earth. He will not leave the Body of Christ in the dark. God sent Jonah to Nineveh to warn the people to repent if they wanted to avoid judgment. God sent Noah to build a boat to save the world. Unfortunately no one listened. God sent Joseph to tell the Egyptians that a famine was coming, and Israel was saved as well because of Joseph's faithfulness. God sent John to prepare the way for Jesus' ministry. Likewise, God is on the verge of the greatest outpouring of His Spirit that the world has ever seen; but we must be prepared, equipped, and activated for His end-time work. Ambassadors must be sent to proclaim the good news of the Kingdom and equip the saints for the work of the ministry.

I am [ambassador] [*to the marketplace*]...*for Christ Jesus* (Philemon 9b RSV).

As you begin to understand the God Factor, it will give you the edge you need in the workplace. Your life at work will begin to take on a whole new meaning.

God goes to work with you and is wanting to bless you and use you for His Kingdom purposes. Your work is more than just about taking home a paycheck; it is your mission field. Instead of saying, "Thank God it is Friday," you are about to say, "I cannot wait for Monday." Why? Monday is the day you reenter your mission field. Maybe you need a whole new perspective on your work. Do you perceive your work as a chore that you have to do each week to provide for your family, or do you see it as an opportunity to bring God's Kingdom into your workplace?

I believe that revival is coming to the marketplace *and the Church had better get ready for the harvest that will be generated when God's saints begin to march in unison with God's vision*! Are you starting to sense the calling on your life? Have you realized that you have a dual anointing as a king and as a priest? Do you understand that you are a full-time minister, whether you are behind a pulpit or a desk? God is releasing His new revelation. It seems to me that we are seeing the beginning of this strategic movement of the saints in the workplace. God is stirring the nest, pushing the saints out of the confines of the church into the marketplaces of the world.

2. *Saints will be equipped.*

Not only must we receive this new revelation of God, but it is essential that we be trained and equipped in how to implement this revelation. We all know that Jesus is coming again for His Bride—the Church. However, before that can happen we must reform our churches into training and equipping centers where the saints are prepared to take their place in the world. God can shout a message from the rooftops, but if you do not respond to the message, then change will not occur. In order for this message to be activated, we have to have places where the saints of God can be trained and then released.

In these training centers the saints must receive the following training:

- How to bring in the harvest of souls on our jobs.

- How to start prayer evangelism meetings in workplaces, schools, neighborhoods, etc.

- How to do the works of Jesus—healing the sick, casting out devils, preaching a Kingdom message (with wonders and miracles following).

- How to disciple others.

And much, much more....

We must be trained and equipped! We must be ready! For the "flood of souls" is coming. Noah started preparing for the flood long before the flood ever came. Likewise, we must start getting prepared now for the new "flood of souls" that is about to enter God's Church. We must be equipped *now*. We must build training centers *now*. For the "flood" is coming!

3. *Saints will be released*

In the first few chapters, I spoke about the importance of the roles of the prophet and apostle in God's end-time Church. As our team of marketplace ministers preach and teach around the world regarding the Saints movement, also known as the Marketplace movement, we rarely leave a meeting or a region without releasing and activating the saints in that region by the laying on of hands and personal prophecy.

Why is this stirring and releasing so important? If a salesman built excitement in you for his product, but never gave you the opportunity to make the purchase, you would feel you had been slighted or had missed something. It is like a preacher telling you about the saving power of Jesus, but never giving you an opportunity to accept Christ in your life. Teaching with revelation, without activation, is simply missing the mark.

Laying on of Hands

As they ministered to the Lord, and fasted, the Holy Ghost said, Separate me Barnabas and Saul for the work whereunto I have called them. And when they had fasted and prayed, and laid their hands on them, they sent them away (Acts 13:2-3).

Laying on of hands is a key component in releasing the Christian into his or her calling. When you lay your hands on someone, the same power and revelation in you is released onto that person. However, there is one stipulation—the individual must be ready to receive. Both Barnabas and Saul had prepared themselves with fasting and prayer. They had been with the Lord. They knew the heartbeat of God. When the men of God laid hands on them, they were ready to receive from the Lord.

So, as the elders of the church laid hands on the men of God, a "release and motivational" anointing was imparted unto them. I have been in meetings where we have "laid hands" on a thousand people at a time, by faith releasing a corporate anointing on a large group. But if time allows, I prefer to lay hands on one at a time. There is nothing like the direct, personal touch. The laying on of hands is a powerful biblical method of releasing and activating the saints into their full-time ministry (as *marketplace ministers*).

Personal Prophecy

But he that prophesieth speaketh unto men to edification, and exhortation, and comfort (1 Corinthians 14:3).

Besides the power of the laying on of hands, personal prophecy is another key component for activating and releasing the saints. Personal prophecy is meant to edify, exhort, and comfort the Christian. God will speak through His fivefold ministers. He may speak into your life about a "heart's desire" for the future or about a situation in which you simply need encouragement. If this former Baptist boy can receive prophecy, then so can you. As God took me on a path to understand the role and function of each fivefold ministry office, only then did I start to understand that each office is needed in God's Church to bring the Body of Christ to the "fullness" of the Lord. I pray that you keep filtering your beliefs, not on man's ideas, but on the Word of God.

Over the years, I have begun to see the power and importance of a clear prophetic word from the Lord spoken into another person's life. It can sometimes make the difference between life and death. Prophetic utterance is a key component in releasing and activating the saints into the work of the Lord.

At meetings our prophetic team puts the messages we speak over people on audio tape. Why? First, we encourage the Christian to listen to the tape over and over again to hear the heartbeat of God in the prophetic message. Secondly, we want to protect our team from false interpretations of the words spoken over someone's life. Having the message on tape benefits both the giver and the receiver of the word.

Saints Come Marching In

When I lived in New Orleans, Louisiana many years ago, the song "When The Saints Go Marching In!" was played many times a day in the old French quarter. I believe God is watching from Heaven, waiting for this song to be played; but it will go something like this: "When the Saints Go Marching Into the Marketplace." Yes, God is releasing His "priests in the Parliament." *Marketplace ministers* are starting to sense their priestly call, realizing their work is their mission field. We do not have to go to a foreign nation to be a missionary. *When we walk into our workplaces on Monday morning, we will have entered our mission field.*

Endnote

1. Dr. Marcus Hester, *How to Finish the Job* (Chicago, Illinois: Hester International Publications, 1999), 23.

Chapter 11

KINGDOM WISDOM CENTERS

Wisdom is the principal thing; therefore get wisdom: and with all thy getting get understanding (Proverbs 4:7).

As God sends out "priests in the Parliament," we are going to need God's wisdom to finish the job. How will we witness to our coworkers? How will we share Christ in our schools? How will we bring the Kingdom of God to our neighborhoods? How will we bring in the end-time harvest of souls from the marketplace? It is going to take God's wisdom.

I believe that we must raise up centers where people will be taught how to effectively handle their finances as well as introduce them to the great opportunities that exist for spiritual and financial investments. Also, in these centers I have a dream that anointed men and women of God will be instructed in the Kingdom of God, and many will be released and sent out with Divine purpose in their heart, freshly anointed for the task. God is raising up within the local church, men and women who are gifted and experienced in business and the ministry. They will be able to help train future ministry leaders into their priestly role, enabling them to assist in the increase of the Kingdom of God and to successfully disciple the new converts. This Joseph/Daniel company of marketplace leaders is springing forth all over the world. It is time the Church recognizes these *marketplace ministers* who are sitting now in the pews of our local churches. They are a great resource for training and equipping the Body of Christ for the workplace.

Then [Jesus] *said to them, "The harvest truly is great, but the laborers are few* [marketplace ministers]*; therefore pray the Lord of the harvest to send out laborers* [marketplace ministers] *into His harvest"* (Luke 10:2 NKJV).

Jesus never had a problem with the harvest. The harvest was always ripe. He did not say to pray for the harvest. He said that we need to pray for more laborers. One of the main purposes of marketplace "ambassadors" is to recruit, train, and release laborers into the fields to work. The harvest is great, but the laborers (*marketplace ministers*) are few.

Releasing Great Power to Get Souls

And with great power gave the apostles witness of the resurrection of the Lord Jesus: and great grace was upon them all (Acts 4:33).

As I mentioned earlier, one of my greatest joys as a minister (priest) and businessman (king) is helping others discover their identity in Christ and their dual callings in the workplace. Another joy of mine is informing the Body of Christ that we live in a period of great opportunity to gather in souls for the Kingdom of God. How will the souls of the world come to the Church? Do you want to hear some good news? The souls of the world are already right there on our jobs, in our neighborhoods, and at our schools. We live and breathe in our harvest field every day. It is a matter of opening our spiritual eyes to the harvest field around us.

Say not ye, there are yet four months, and then cometh harvest? Behold, I say unto you, Lift up your eyes and look on the [work] *fields; for they are white **already** to harvest* (John 4:35, emphasis added).

We must begin to see our surroundings at work like Jesus saw them—*a harvest field!* It is time to take our "blinders" off. Are you going to your work today, or are you going to your mission field? Are you going to school today, or are you going to your harvest field? It is a matter of how you perceive your work, your school, or your neighborhood. We have to start "seeing" like Jesus sees. We need the eyes of Jesus to see the great opportunities that exist all around us. We must see and feel the hurts and pains of those around us at work. We must visualize the eternal destinies of our coworkers who do not know Christ. "Oh Lord, give us the compassionate eyes of Jesus."

New Dimensions of Wisdom in God's Kingdom

Wisdom is the principal thing; therefore get wisdom: and with all thy getting get understanding (Proverbs 4:7).

God is raising up a new breed of leaders who will help bring souls into the Kingdom. They will be *marketplace ministers* who have discovered the uniqueness and power of their calling. These new believers will need places to be trained in this calling. These centers of which I have spoken can be places where we will:

1. *Produce leaders who walk in "wonders and miracles."*

And Stephen, full of faith and power, did great wonders and miracles among the people (Acts 6:8).

As members of the Body of Christ start stepping out in faith as workplace ambassadors for Christ, then watch out! God is looking for some modern-day "Peters" who will step out of the boat to walk on water at work, at school, and in their homes. Yes, "wonders and miracles" will follow you, too.

What are "wonders and miracles," and why do we need them? First of all, a "wonder and miracle" is any supernatural act of God working in someone's life. For example, a "wonder and miracle" may be when you pray for your coworker's marriage to be healed and then God heals that relationship. A "wonder and miracle" may be when you are asked to pray for a healing at school (sprained ankle) and God performs the healing through your prayers. The point I am trying to make is this: A "wonder and miracle" is not some mystical event. A "wonder and miracle" may simply be a Christian speaking a word of encouragement (word of prophecy) into a coworker's life. Who can walk in "wonders and miracles"? Everyone can! We all have the same Holy Spirit within us—so you too can walk in "wonders and miracles" in the marketplace.

But why do we need "wonders and miracles" in the workplace? As I discussed earlier, many times people's felt needs have to be met before their hearts open to their greater need for eternal life. When God performs a "wonder and miracle" through you, He is simply saying to the one who received the miracle, "Yes, I have sent this messenger to you. I am confirming their words with My 'wonders and miracles,' so that you will know how much I care for you and want to change your life." God is validating you as a witness, proving that God has sent you. Once these "wonders and miracles" are performed through you, then trust me, the workplace will be talking about you. "Did you hear what happened at lunch? Jane prayed for Mary and Mary's arm was healed." You will be the talk of the office. Hearts will be opened up for you to now share the love of Christ. God wants to validate you at work. God wants to validate you at school. God wants to validate you in your neighborhood…with "wonders and miracles" following your words.

> *And Jesus went about all the cities and villages, teaching in their synagogues, and preaching the gospel of the kingdom, and healing every sickness and every disease among the people* (Matthew 9:35).

Many "wonders and signs" occur within the nuclear (local) church, but during the current Marketplace movement, a majority of the "wonders and miracles" will be exhibited in the marketplace (extended church). Many Christians come up to me after my meetings and say, "Dr. Hester, how can I see more 'wonders and miracles' in my life, especially at work?" I try to encourage them to first realize that the Body of Christ is living in a time of much grace, enabling them to walk in the supernatural. But I also point out that this grace is uniquely being poured out in the marketplace where they are praying for the felt needs of the lost. They can have faith and know that the "wonders and miracles" will follow them…as they do the works of the Lord in the marketplace.

2. *Produce leaders who walk in compassion and the servant spirit of the Lord.*

> *But when He saw the multitudes, He was moved with compassion on them, because they fainted, and were scattered abroad, as sheep having no shepherd* (Matthew 9:36).

Jesus had compassion. He was not moved by greed or self-seeking motives. Jesus was moved by His love for people. For the Christian to be successful in this next move of God within the workplace, the love of God has to be his primary motive. Remember that *how* you speak to others is just as important as *what* you say to them.

We must see through the eyes of Jesus, the same eyes that viewed all men as worthy of His Father's love. Believe me, it is only by the power of love that we will see changes in the workplace. The way we see our coworkers must change.

We should see them with the love of Christ. If we show them love then we will be showing them God! Remember, the testimony of your life will be the only Jesus that many people will ever see. God's end-time *marketplace ministers* will walk in the love and compassion of God. Let's reverse the misguided view the world has of God because of the fundamentalism and legalism that exists in the Body of Christ. As we have been touched by the love of God we can go forth as an army and convince others of His mighty love.

> *Yet it shall not be so among you; but whoever desires to become great among you shall be your servant. And whoever of you desires to be first shall be slave of all. For even the Son of Man did not come to be served, but to serve, and to give His life a ransom for many* (Mark 10:43-45 NKJV).

God's end-time *marketplace ministers* will walk not only in the love and compassion of God, but also in the spirit of a servant. In the workplace, many people are trying to work their way up the corporate ladder. Nothing is wrong with this desire, but the way the goal is achieved is the problem. If, in your ascent up this ladder, you are stepping on the man or woman above you or using ungodly techniques to get promoted, you will reap evil things in your life. Many are reaching their goals, but in return they are losing their families, children, and peace of mind. God has a better way! Jesus' model of leadership was rooted in servanthood. Servanthood is simply an attitude of living in the service of others, rather than thinking of ourselves all the time. Yes, there is a balance between meeting our own needs and meeting the needs of those around us. We know that we are not put here on earth to live just for ourselves, but for others (coworkers, classmates, and neighbors) around us. This is one of the great keys of the marketplace—serving others. By the power of Kingdom servanthood, we will rise to new levels of influence and effectiveness. Just ask Joseph.

Humble yourselves before the Lord, and He will lift you up [give you a promotion] (James 4:10 NIV).

If you want to be promoted on your job, then be the best servant at work. For many years I was in charge of managing a sales force for Dupont. As a regional manager, I sometimes had to fire people. This was always a difficult task. But I found great joy in giving an employee a promotion or raise at the annual review period. In making my decision, I looked over the employee's ability to meet goals and objectives, but I looked also at attitude—whether the employee had a humble and servant heart. I discovered that when the person walked in the spirit of the servant, the sales numbers always seemed to line up with their attitude. Giving that employee a promotion was easy for me. It was not simply about job skills, but about the ability to work with others and to display a servant's heart.

God's *marketplace ministers* will walk with the compassion of Jesus and the spirit of the servant. They will realize that it is not all about them, but about their ability to love and serve others.

3. *Produce leaders who will equip and train others.*

In order to pull in God's end-time harvest of souls, the Church will need human resources to finish the job. We will need leaders who can train ministers. One of the main defining features of these centers will be the ability to reproduce ministry leaders who can be sent out to train others in their various churches.

Fivefold ministry leaders will have the responsibility of training the Body of Christ to bring in the harvest for the Kingdom. These fivefold trainers (*marketplace ministers*) will have the wisdom of God to train, equip, and release the saints of God. In the Kingdom Wisdom Centers we need preachers to cast the vision of the Marketplace movement and trainers who will roll up their sleeves and train the future marketplace ministers. Jesus did not just preach a sermon and leave town. He preached a sermon and then showed the people how to do what He did. He taught by example—what I call the "follow me" principle. These centers will be training and equipping centers to show people how to do the work in the marketplace.

Not only will these centers have local and regional training facilities to equip our future marketplace ministers, but I envision that they will be resource centers for all kinds of information (books, tapes, articles, videos, etc.). *Marketplace ministers* will be able to utilize these powerful resource tools for their spiritual growth and marketplace acumen.

4. Conference and network with others.

Again, the kingdom of heaven is like unto a net [network], *that was cast into the sea, and gathered of every kind* (Matthew 13:47).

These centers can also become places where key men and women of God with a calling to be *marketplace ministers* will meet other men and women of God with similar callings. God is networking the right people together to accomplish His end-time work. *Marketplace ministers* will meet their counterparts through local and regional conferences. These local, regional, and international meetings will be strategic in bringing people together to strategize on how to increase God's purposes in the marketplace all around the world.

Preparing for the Harvest

Through these resource centers, people will be able to identify and develop their callings. Godly men and women full of wisdom and character will be able to train others and assist them in bringing in God's end-time harvest of souls for the marketplace.

In preparation for the great opportunities that exist all around us I believe that the Church must get ready. Both *marketplace managers* (kings) and *marketplace ministers* (priests) are being positioned now in God's Church in order to facilitate the training and releasing of the saints into the workplace.

Are you one of God's end-time ministers of finance? Are you one of God's end-time marketplace ministers? Are you ready to be used by God to be a blessing to His Church? Are you a wealth builder for the Kingdom? Are you a soul winner for the Kingdom? Are you ready to walk in your dual calling as a *marketplace manager* and a *marketplace minister*?

What a powerful opportunity God has presented to the Body of Christ. We can be both "kings and priests" in the marketplace. We are all full-time wealth builders for the Kingdom, but at the same time, we are "full-time" ministers of the gospel. We do not have to choose. We can have it all! God wants us to have it all. As we move on into the last section (God's Expecting Church), my prayer is that you will get a revelation of what God is about to do in the marketplace. I pray that your faith level will be raised so that you are expecting God to do a great work within the marketplace.

> *But without faith* [expectancy] *it is impossible to please Him: for he that cometh to God must believe that He is, and that He is a rewarder of them that diligently seek Him* (Hebrews 11:6).

Section Four

GOD'S EXPECTING CHURCH

...Will You Walk in Your Calling?

Chapter 12

PRAYER INC.

Jabez cried out to the God of Israel, "Oh, that You would bless me and enlarge my territory! Let Your hand be with me, and keep me from harm so that I will be free from pain." And God granted his request (1 Chronicles 4:10 NIV).

One of the greatest cries of the marketplace leader is that God will bless him and enlarge his territory. He or she asks God to make business transactions go smoothly and to help the business continue to grow. Who does not want that type of prayer? However, two key ingredients must be in place to make this happen. First of all, you need to have a relationship with God and secondly, you need to pray. Prayer creates a spirit of expectancy in a business like nothing else can. Prayer in the workplace creates an environment of faith that all is going to be all right. Prayer does change things.

Church leaders for centuries have realized that the majority of their ministry success has been because their endeavors were started with prayer, continued in prayer, were maintained in prayer, and grew in prayer. Marketplace leaders are beginning to take hold of the power of prayer and incorporate it into their businesses. For example:

Since hiring his mother as a combination bookkeeper/intercessor in 1995, Victor Eagan said his business has prospered. The Detroit-area orthodontist said intercession also promotes a peaceful atmosphere.

A Dallas-based ministry turned its focus from supporting missionaries to training "marketplace intercessors." Though Beth Alves, president of Intercessors

International, has prayed regularly for businesses since 1984, she said interest is growing.

Jennifer Kaplan of the Equal Employment Opportunity Commission (EEOC) said employers are increasingly concerned about making reasonable accommodations for the faith of employees (prayer).

In the last few years, we have seen major Fortune 500 companies allow company employees to conduct prayer meetings at work (American Airlines, Wal-Mart, and IBM). Corporate America is seeing the benefits of allowing prayer in the workplace. Businesses and marketplace leaders are seeing the "bottom lines" improve due to the power of prayer. Jabez was a wealthy business owner who knew the power of prayer. Our business leaders need to recognize that powerful truth as well.

Prayer Has Always Been a Part of the Business World

When men tell you to consult mediums and spiritists, who whisper and mutter, should not a people inquire of their God? (Isaiah 8:19 NIV)

Businesspeople for centuries have consulted the spirit world for wisdom on making decisions. They have prayed for the rain to fall and for their crops to grow. They have made idols to make their finances increase. Today, we see law enforcement offices consult psychic profilers to solve a case. Television is bombarded with psychic mediums trying to help people contact their dead relatives. The spirit world these people are dabbling in is the devil's world. The devil may answer your prayers for a season, but he will always turn on you and cause pain in your life. Prayer is our secret weapon of power, but only when we pray to the true and living God.

Years ago, when I was exercising at a health club, a man came up to me asking me things about keeping in shape and what he should eat to be healthy. I gave him a few suggestions on a workout plan and a simple nutritional regimen to follow. What if this man truly believed that the road to good health was just sitting on his couch all day eating ice cream? What if he ignored my advice and was certain in his mind that he would lose weight with his plan? What if this man was very sincere and in his mind was one hundred percent correct? He would quickly find out he was wrong.

Many times in business, we are convinced our decisions and methods are one hundred percent correct, but in reality they are completely off the mark. We may sincerely believe that we have taken the right action steps, but we can be completely wrong. In a speech I made to a group in Florida recently, I stated, "You can be sincere in what you believe, but still be sincerely wrong. Truth is not what you believe, but truth is what *is*." When it comes to implementing prayer in the workplace, we must be sure we are praying to the right God. We must be sure our relationship with Him is in good standing. We cannot just *hope* all is right (being sincere), but we must *know* (walking in the truth) that all is right.

If you do not know for sure that you have a right relationship with God, here are a few steps to take:

Realize that Heaven is a free gift—it is not earned or deserved. It is an act of grace given to all who will receive it.

Man is a sinner and he cannot save himself. All of us have missed the mark in our lives. As much as we would like to believe that we can do something to erase our mistakes, we cannot.

God is love, but God is righteous as well. Many of us would agree that God is love, but at the same time…God is just and He must punish sin. So, how do we receive this free gift of eternal life (securing a right relationship with God)?

Jesus Christ is the answer. Jesus Christ came to earth and lived a sinless life, but while on earth…He died on the cross to pay the penalty for our sins and rose from the grave to purchase a place for us in Heaven.

Faith is the key to receiving this free gift of Jesus Christ. Faith is the key that opens the door to Heaven. By faith you can ask Jesus into your heart to forgive you of your sins.

Some of you have known God, but have not experienced Him in a long time. Some of you desire to pray to God and long to know your prayers are being heard. But you just have not taken the steps to having a right relationship with God. If this is you, you can get your life right with your God right now by saying this simple prayer:

"Lord Jesus Christ, I know I am a sinner and do not deserve eternal life. I believe You died and rose from the grave to purchase a place in Heaven for me. Lord Jesus, come into my life; take control of my life; forgive my sins and save me. I repent of my sins and now place my trust in You for my salvation. I accept the free gift of eternal life."

What Is Prayer?

One day Jesus was praying in a certain place. When He finished, one of His disciples said to Him, "Lord, teach us to pray, just as John taught his disciples." He said to them, "When you pray, say: 'Father, hallowed be Your name, Your kingdom come. Give us each day our daily bread. Forgive us our sins, for we also forgive everyone who sins against us. And lead us not into temptation' " (Luke 11:1-4 NIV).

Jesus gave His disciples a model prayer. There are many aspects to this prayer, but the bottom line of prayer is twofold. First, we are to honor God with our prayers. Secondly, we are to pray His will—which is that His Kingdom will come on this earth according to *His* plan, not ours. But prayer in its simplest form is our communicating with God. We talk to God and God talks to us. Prayer is the tool for our relationship to God. Prayer is not hard; it is easy. It is not a religious act; it is simply conversation with God.

Do we have to make decisions every day in the marketplace? Do we need help in deciding when to buy or when to sell? Could we use some help from someone who already knows all the answers? Well, we might call the God helpline—1-800-HelpGod—24 hours a day and 7 days a week. We might e-mail Him at www.helpmeGod.com. No, we do not need a phone or the Internet. We can go directly to God anytime or anyplace with the powerful tool God gives to all of us—the gift of prayer. It is even easier than picking up the phone or sending an e-mail.

Do not be anxious about anything, but in everything, by prayer and petition,
with thanksgiving, present your requests to God (Philippians 4:6 NIV).

Anytime and anywhere, God is there to help you in business. Prayer is the tool to your connection with God. You don't have to fast 40 days and 40 nights to pray to God. You don't have to sell all you have and give the money to the poor. All you have to do is turn your heart toward God. Invite Him into the circumstances of your life as you ask for His help. What an edge the Christian businessman has over his competition! Through prayer, you can always be one step ahead. So what is prayer? Prayer is you talking to God and God talking to you. Prayer is seeking God who is more knowing and powerful than you are and letting Him be the CEO of your life and business.

Hearing the Voice of God

And it [success in the workplace] *shall come to pass, if thou shalt hearken diligently unto the voice* [hear God's voice] *of the Lord thy God, to observe and to do all His commandments* [obey] *which I command thee this day, that the Lord thy God will set thee on high above all nations of the earth* (Deuteronomy 28:1).

Working with a Fortune 500 company for many years, I discovered that many businessmen and women think more about one thing than any other. This one thing is achieving success! Success might mean different things to different people, but being successful in whatever they do is first on their minds. The question is how do you achieve success? I can give the world's answer (just go to any bookstore and pick up the many books on the topic), but I want to give you what God says on the subject. Success can be broken down into two categories. First, one must be able to hear God's voice; secondly, one must obey what he hears. It is that simple! However, in my 20 years of ministry, I have discovered that sometimes people need help in learning how to hear the voice of the Lord. If you are having problems in this area, you are not alone.

My sheep hear My voice, and I know them, and they follow Me (John 10:27).

Hearing the voice of the Lord is a learned process. As my three children grew up, they learned how to recognize my voice. For example, if I was in a room with a group and I called out to one of my children, that child would instantly distinguish my voice from the others in the room. In the same way, if one of my children needed help, as a parent I would know immediately if this was my child or someone else's, just by the sound of the scream. In both these cases, the learning process of recognizing one another's voices took time and practice. In our Kingdom Wisdom Centers, we spend a great deal of time training our marketplace ministers in how to hear the voice of the Lord. Here are a few practical guidelines on hearing from the Lord:

Avoid distractions. The active mind will always be the greatest obstacle to hearing the Holy Spirit. Just as we make business appointments, we need to make appointments with God (without any distractions). One lady told me, "Cancelled prayer will wear you out." What a true statement! If we miss prayer and thrust ourselves into the day, we seem not to accomplish much. However, if we put God and our prayer time first, then He redeems our time for the rest of the day. Specify a place and time to pray. When you pray, you must be totally focused on the Lord.

Respect the Holy Spirit. Treat the Holy Spirit like the Person He really is. Reverence Him. No one likes being used, including God. Approach Him first with thanksgiving and praise (Psalm 100). We should always take time to thank Him for answered prayers. God can't resist a thankful heart.

Pray for the increase of the Kingdom. Ask the Holy Spirit what is on His mind. Wait upon the Lord for Him to speak to you. Once you have prayed what is on God's heart, then bring up your own needs and questions.

Pray about one thing at a time. When praying, most people mistakenly ask God for wisdom and direction concerning several subjects at one time. Not being specific leads to confusion, because when the Holy Spirit speaks to you through a picture, or by words, or in some other manner in prayer, it is difficult to know which subject He is addressing. It is important to ask Him only one question at a time, and take time to listen for a few minutes.

Pray with expectation. Many people have been taught to pray in generalities, by giving a long list of needs to God. This type of prayer is necessary when interceding for needs of various people, but not when seeking God for specific guidance. We must remember that prayer is a two-way conversation. In order to hear from God, you must be convinced that God is going to talk to you. Without expectation and belief that you are going to hear an answer, why pray?

Don't try to persuade God to change His mind. This is one of the most frustrating lessons to learn. Even though we don't like to admit it, sometimes our mind is made up more than we realize, and we go back again and again to the Lord, to obtain the answer we desire. The difficulty is that we want the Lord to confirm what we want, more than we want what He wants.

Don't demand God to be sensational. Many people have God in a sensational box in their minds. They think anything that God does will be loud, mind staggering, and will leave one in an altered state for days. Like Moses, many are waiting for God to speak to them through their "burning bush." This kind of thinking is contrary to fellowship and intimacy with the Holy Spirit. In fact, when the Holy Spirit communes and speaks to us, it can almost be described as subtle. His gentle prompting, quiet nudges, and silent illuminations never come with force, but must be reached out for, accepted, and embraced. He is a gentleman! We have to train ourselves to recognize and trust His still small voice. We have to take the time to fellowship with the Holy Spirit.

Be focused in your prayers. One of the most difficult things to do is to pray about something when you are emotionally involved in it. Emotions cannot be avoided but they must be directed. As a businessman, many times I have to make decisions with time restraints. I know a wrong decision can cost the company thousands of dollars. Or better yet, my right decision can add thousands to the company's bottom line. Like many, I sometimes let my emotions get in the way of hearing the voice of the Lord. When it comes to a decision, instead of hearing God, many Christians weigh the pros and cons, weigh the advantages and disadvantages, and make the decision based on human reasoning and not in obedience to a "nod" from the Holy Spirit. Focused prayer will bring the answer you need.

Trust your first impressions. The mind of man is quick to defile the mind of the Holy Spirit, simply through the reasoning process. When you are seeking God for His direction, the first impression is often the most accurate. Soon the mind begins to analyze and bring forth the pros and cons, and then confusion sets in.

God speaks once. Asked how he knew he had heard from God, a famous evangelist told a friend of mine, "God speaks only one time." The statement is true. God is not confused. He doesn't have two or three wills. He speaks as a King. He doesn't need to weigh a decision, or need time to think about it. However, He is merciful, and when we pray sincerely for clarity, He will confirm His will to us.

Don't take yourself too seriously. Trying too hard and taking yourself too seriously can often constrict the flow of the Holy Spirit. The harder you try, the less room there is for God to get through. Laugh at yourself. Don't be religious, but love God. I remember an event that happened when I was teaching my middle son to swim. The harder he tried to swim, the more he would sink to the bottom of the pool. After a second's thought I came up with a new strategy. I taught my son to float— to just remain still in the water (not trying so hard). Once my son learned how to float in the water, he learned to swim within a short period of time. Don't take yourself so seriously, but do take God seriously.

Don't be a perfectionist. The bondage of perfectionism robs us of enjoying God, and constricts us from hearing clearly. We Christians have not been afforded the luxury of the freedom to fail. Much of the teaching from various Christian circles implies that we must not fail God in anything. However, although we don't intentionally fail God, we have to realize that He leaves room for "missing" His voice. In our listening to God, sometimes the Holy Spirit will say, "Try again." In our most sincere efforts to hear the voice of God, we miss it at times. But praise God, there is freedom to fail in the Kingdom of God.

Get to know God intimately. Never use God as a formula to plug into, in order to get what you are asking for. Don't separate your relationship with God from the petitions and wisdom you seek from Him. All life flows out of relationship. He wants your relationship and fellowship with Him to be enhanced daily. He can easily redeem mistakes. What He wants is the reins of your heart.

Trust even when you don't understand. I have had a number of experiences where I knew I had heard the Lord, but I couldn't interpret what He was saying until months later when I looked back at the situation. This is where simple trust comes in.[1]

So if we want to achieve true success, we must be able to "hear the voice" of the Lord and then obey what He tells us. God speaks clearly when we endeavor to obey Him.

Corporate Prayer Covering

Spiritual leaders for centuries have known that prayer can help their ministries grow. They have realized that strategic prayer can be one of the key factors in achieving success in their ministries.[2] However, businessmen and women are just starting to realize that prayer can give them the edge at work as well. Prayer, another God Factor, is helping them have more success than they ever could have realized.

Business owners have even gone as far as to hire "full-time prayer intercessors" to cover their business efforts in prayer.

Have you ever you felt a calling to pray for your coworkers? Have you ever considered hiring a full-time business prayer intercessor for your company? Let us now look at some steps you may take if you desire to be a prayer intercessor at your workplace (forming a marketplace prayer group) and/or hire a full-time prayer leader for your business.

Called to Prayer in the Workplace

Many have felt called to pray at work (start a prayer group), but do not know how to walk in that calling. Here are some ideas:

You do not need permission to pray. Prayer is something you can do walking down the hall or driving in your car. You can start just by praying for the various needs of the business. From praying for your boss, to praying for your company to meet certain business quotas, you can start by simply praying wherever you are. *However, please do not pray when you should be working.* One of the worst things you can do to hurt your testimony at work is to pray when you should be working. There are times to pray (your breaks, lunchtime, etc.), but work when you need to work and pray when it is time to pray.

Identify a partner. One of your prayers might be praying that God will help you identify someone else at work with whom you can pray. "Two are better than one; because they have a good reward for their labour" (Eccl. 4:9). Your prayers are more effective if two or three can pray together. As you start praying this prayer (keeping your spiritual antennae up), then shortly God will put in your path someone else with whom you can possibly team up with. As I have talked to many marketplace ministers around the world, I have discovered that God has that second person already planted in your workplace. Through prayer He will reveal that person to you.

Start posting the results. In a prayer journal, you and your prayer team need to start posting your answers to prayer. Share them with the group to encourage one another. As you start recording your results (for your group's information only), you will see God moving through your prayers. Your faith level will increase with each newly answered prayer.

Start meeting regularly. Keeping a consistent schedule is important. It is important to the group's success. Just as we need to meet with the Lord each day in our personal prayer times, we also need to keep a consistent meeting time for our marketplace prayer group.

Begin a Felt Need Prayer Evangelism Group. The first prayer team consists mainly of Christians who are praying for the company and each others' needs. However, the purpose of meeting together in this manner is to start ministering to the unchurched of your workplace. They too will want to experience the power of prayer in their lives. Let us not forget that our ultimate goal is to bring in the harvest of souls from the workplace. We are not talking here about forming another Christian prayer group at work, but rather about laying a foundation of prayer at work (Christian Workplace Prayer Teams), so that in turn, we can start bringing in the harvest of souls from the workplace. Later in this chapter, I will give you some additional steps for starting and conducting this type of prayer evangelism meeting.

Hiring a Company Prayer Intercessor

Many business owners have realized that prayer can help their business grow, but do not know how to recruit or identify a company prayer intercessor. Consider the following:

You have to start praying yourself. Hiring a prayer leader is important, but the chief intercessor for your company is *you*! If you are the CEO of your company, then God holds you responsible for praying for your business. However, that does not mean that God cannot bring you help in this area. For example, as the president of my company, I have others, such as a sales manager and a marketing director, who help me in my business. Each manager has different responsibilities and duties; however, when all is said and done, I still have the ultimate responsibility for sales and marketing. You may hire a prayer intercessor for your company, but as owner or CEO, you still have the ultimate responsibility for the prayer covering of your business. So, if you are looking to hire a prayer intercessor so you do not have to pray any longer, you have missed the point. Trust me; God will not let that go on for too long. However, if you are looking for a prayer intercessor to help you in your prayer efforts, then God will always work through pure motives. So first you need to develop a strong prayer life yourself. You will always be the Chief Prayer Intercessor of your company.

Pray for the prayer leader to come forth. Start asking God to identify someone who can help you in this area. God in His timing will eventually put the right prayer leader in your path. Let God lead you in your selection. It might be somebody whom you least expect. Walk in God's timing. A good intercessor can be a great blessing to a company, but a wrong intercessor put in position can do great harm. As I have talked with many company owners, I have discovered that this process of finding the right company intercessor sometimes is very difficult. Our ministry has a special division whose purpose is to pray with and counsel business owners who want to hire a prayer intercessor for their company. In the future we will also have a "pool" of proven marketplace intercessors from which to select.

Set your new prayer leader in place. Since this is a new position for many companies, communicating the prayer leader's responsibilities to the others in the company will be critical. Some people will not understand his or her role. Others might want to use this person as their personal pray warrior. It is important that you establish boundaries. Having an employment agreement with your prayer leader (whether a voluntary or paid position) is just as important as the employment agreement you have with all other employees. In this agreement, all the terms and conditions of your working relationship must be made clear.

Establish communication and trust. Over the years, many people may have said they would pray for you and your business. While these prayers are good, rarely are they very effective—because they are general rather than specific prayers. To be an effective prayer leader, one must know what is going on in the business. For example, the prayer intercessor may need to know potential problem areas, future directions that the company might be heading in, and sometimes intimate details that only the CEO of the company may know. As you can see, just for this reason alone, selecting the right prayer intercessor is important. Not only must the prayer leader know how to pray (walking in God's authority to pray for you and your company), but he or she must be trustworthy in handling vital company information. If this new relationship is going to be successful, important information must flow both ways between you and your intercessor. Lines of communication must be open. I encourage intercessors to meet weekly with their employers if time permits. Relationships take time to develop. However, for both the CEO and prayer intercessor to reach their goals and objectives, strong lines of communication and trust must be developed.

Form a company prayer strategy. Just as you have a business plan for your company, both you and your prayer leader must set a company prayer plan in place. Set goals and implement action steps. One of the main objectives of a business plan is to give the company leadership a road map to follow. Likewise, a company prayer plan should work hand in hand with the company's current business plan. The prayer plan should add a spiritual dimension to the existing plan, thus helping the business reach its goals and objectives within a shorter period of time. Most businessmen and women govern their success by seeing results. They want to see growth or progress. Likewise, the company's prayer strategies should produce results, and the goal and objectives of the prayer plan should be measurable as well.

Decide on a salary. Many companies will have volunteer prayer leaders, but some will see the value of this new staff position and want to hire this person full time (putting them on the payroll). You can give them an annual salary or a percentage of increased business. Whatever you decide (paying for a prayer leader or recruiting a volunteer), a good company prayer leader is worth his or her weight in gold. I am seeing a growing trend of hiring staff prayer intercessors (who are on the payroll). I believe in the future, the companies that want the edge at work will be adding this new position to their staffs. The God Factor (prayer) will propel the company that employs it leaps ahead of their competition. Times are changing! The workplace is changing! Methods of doing business are changing. Do you have your prayer intercessor in place in your company?

Workplace Prayer Evangelism

Let us look now at how we can be more effective as prayer evangelists at work. The foundational prayer group is important, but eventually we will want to start a Felt Need Prayer Evangelism Group. This group is where our lost coworkers will start finding Christ. Before we talk about starting a Felt Need Prayer Evangelism Group, let me give you seven practical steps for winning people to the Lord in your everyday 9-5 workplace environment. I call it lifestyle (or workplace) prayer evangelism.

Build a relationship. Many Christians have relationships only with other Christians. How are we going to tell others about Jesus at work when we do not build a relationship with them? I am not saying that we need to be a part of their immoral actions, but we have to hang out with sinners (like Jesus did) to know them—their hurts, pains, and cares.

> *The Son of Man came eating and drinking, and they say, "Look, a glutton and a winebibber, a friend of tax collectors and sinners!" But wisdom is justified by her children* (Matthew 11:19 NKJV).

Jesus was called many names (glutton and winebibber) and was misunderstood many times. However, Jesus stayed true to His assignment to save the lost (not the religious folks of the church). Jesus hung out with sinners in the workplace. For us to be effective in the workplace, we are going to have to start walking outside of the comfort circles of our Christian friends, and start making friends with sinners.[3]

Identify a "felt need." Felt needs are needs (for example, a physical healing, a relationship problem, a financial matter, etc.) that are important to your coworker, but in reality mask the far greater need of a relationship with God (their eternal need). One of the first steps in getting your coworker's heart turned back to God is to meet his or her felt need.[4]

Pray for the felt need. Now be faithful and begin praying that God will answer the prayer. Let your coworker know that you will be praying. You may say something like this to your coworker, "I am sorry that you hurt your knee playing volleyball this last weekend. You know I am a Christian; do you mind if I pray for your knee to be healed?" I haven't had one person turn me down when I've offered to pray. Rarely does anyone refuse prayer in time of need. Once you get permission, you need to pray daily for God to meet your coworker's felt need.

Pray in Jesus' name. Tell your coworker that you are praying for them in Jesus' name. This is important. When God answers prayer, your coworker will know that no other god than the true and almighty God of the Bible answered his or her prayer. Many people believe in God, but do not believe in the same God of the Bible as you. Make it very clear to your coworker that you will be praying in Jesus' name.

Ask one qualifying question. Once you ask permission to pray for the felt need of your coworker, just ask one more qualifying question. You may say something like, "I will be praying for you, but can you do me one favor? When God answers your prayer, would you just let me know about it?" Then continue to pray and expect God to answer. Periodically, inquire about how things are going. One day that person will come up to you with a "praise report" of how God answered the prayer.

Share Jesus with your coworker. When your coworker has shared the good news of the answered prayer, you will know God has now prepared him or her (opened up their heart) for you to share the gospel. This series of events has shown your workplace friend that God loves him or her, because He has met a felt need.

Take them to church. Once your coworker has accepted Christ, you have to be the one to help in the discipling process. Now, more than ever, be there. Take the new believer to church with you; or, if that is not possible (maybe because of distance), help him or her find a Bible-believing church that is nearby. When we lead others to the Lord, we have a responsibility to help in their Christian growth.

The following scenario might help you get a better understanding of how to share your faith at work through the felt need prayer evangelism method. Bob and his unchurched coworker, Jim, work in the marketing department at the headquarters of a large financial institution. Since their offices are in close proximity on the 20th floor of the building, and they see one another daily, Bob has been building a relationship with Jim over the last two months. Bob and Jim meet in the break room on Monday morning after a long holiday weekend...

Bob says, "How did your weekend go? Did you do any fishing? Did you take the wife and kids with you?" With a gloomy look on his face, Jim responds, "Yes, we went fishing, but I did not catch a thing." Sensing that Jim is sad about something more than just not catching any fish, Bob asks, "Jim, in the last few months, we have gotten a little closer in our relationship. Can you tell me, what is really bothering you?" Jim, with tears in his eyes and head hung down low, murmurs, "I think my wife is going to divorce me." Bob, immediately and with the compassion of Jesus, responds, "Jim, I am so sorry to hear that. What exactly happened?"

Jim goes on to share with Bob how his marriage has been strained for many months; how he and his wife have even seen a marriage counselor, but nothing seems to help. In the break room that morning, Bob spends some time listening to Jim and sharing in Jim's pain. When the conversation is coming to a close Bob quickly says, "Jim, you know I am a Christian and I believe that prayer can change things. Do you mind if I pray for you and your marriage? I will be praying to Jesus that He does a miracle in your life and marriage." Jim looks surprised at first, but doubtfully responds, "Sure, I will give anything a try at this time. Nothing else seems to work."

You may be aware of it already, but let us review what has happened in these series of events with Bob and Jim. Bob has been trying to build a relationship with

Jim over the last few months (step one). As Bob and Jim met in the coffee room Monday morning after a weekend break, Bob sensed that Jim was not his cheerful self. After a few probing questions, Jim started sharing with Bob his concerns about his marriage. A felt need was identified (step two)—Jim's possible divorce from his wife. As Bob listened with empathy to his friend, he did not just end the conversation and walk away, doing nothing. No, Bob closed the conversation by asking Jim if he could pray for him and his marriage in Jesus' name (steps three and four). Bob's job has now just begun! He adds Jim's request to his prayer journal and prays daily that God will touch Jim's marriage—his felt need. However, before Bob and Jim depart from their Monday morning break room scene, Bob asks Jim a qualifying question.

"Jim, could you do me a favor?" Jim responds, "Sure, Bob, what is it?" Bob says, "I will be praying for you and your marriage, and I'm asking you to let me know if things get better with your relationship?" Jim replies, "I will let you know!"

Weeks and months go by. Both Bob and Jim have many projects at work that must be completed on time. One day at work Jim grabs Bob's arm and literally drags him into his office, shutting the door behind them. Jim excitedly says, "Bob, you will not believe what has happened. My marriage is better than it has ever been! My wife and I have started going to church together. I do not know what is happening to me, but I feel different." Bob listens, rejoicing with Jim, and then says, "How did you like church?" Jim says, "I liked it, but I do not understand what the minister meant by having a relationship with God." Bob lovingly asks, "Do you mind if I share with you how you can have a relationship with God?" With Jim's permission, Bob shares the gospel, then leads Jim in the sinner's prayer. Jim becomes a new Christian. In the following weeks, Bob encourages Jim to continue attending church and to start praying for his wife to get saved as well. One Monday morning a few weeks later in the coffee room, Jim grabs Bob, giving him a big hug. "Bob, my wife walked down the aisle yesterday. She accepted Jesus into her heart, too. God is good! Bob, I don't think I ever thanked you, but thank you for praying for me when I needed it most. You really are a true friend!"

What a beautiful ending, for a story than can happen thousands of times a day in the workplaces all around the world. This is marketplace evangelism at its best. However, before we conclude this scenario in the workplace with Bob and Jim, let us evaluate these final steps that Bob took as he led Jim to the Lord. As Bob and Jim were walking out of the break room, Bob asked Jim if he would let him know if things changed for the better with his marriage. Here Bob was exercising step five by asking a qualifying question. As months passed and Bob was praying daily (behind the scenes), one day the opportunity presented itself for Bob to share Jesus with his friend Jim. God had answered Bob's prayer by healing Jim's marriage. As God met this felt need, Jim's heart became open to receive Jesus when Bob shared Christ with him (step six). However, Bob knew that his job was not finished. Bob encouraged Jim to keep attending church (step seven) and offered, if need be, to work out a discipleship plan with him.

Jesus used this method of evangelism many times in the New Testament. By feeding the five thousand (felt need of food)…to healing the blind (felt need of physical healing)…to casting out demons (felt need of deliverance)…Jesus used this felt need style of evangelism. Why? *Because it works!* I believe it will work for you, too, as a workplace minister. You may not yet have a workplace prayer evangelism group started; however, you can be a workplace minister right now wherever you are—*at work*!

Prayer Evangelism Group

We have discussed how you can start and be a part of a Christian Workplace Prayer Group. We have looked at some of the steps that an employer might need to take in hiring a company prayer intercessor. And we have expounded upon how an *individual* Christian can lead others to the Lord at work, by using the felt need prayer evangelism method. As we conclude this chapter on workplace prayer, I would like to give you some helpful steps for starting a Prayer Evangelism Group at work. As we stated earlier, once you establish a Christian Workplace Prayer Group (praying for your coworkers, your boss, and the needs of the other Christian coworkers in your group), this group can be extended into meeting the "felt needs" of others in the workplace. The main purpose of this is to start "casting a net" in your workplace to those coworkers who have not yet discovered the love of Christ. Initially your group can pray and bless one another, but you will eventually want to focus on evangelism as well, bringing the Kingdom of God to your workplace. We have demonstrated how individually you can share Christ at work (the story of Bob and Jim) with this new focused approach. Here are some helps as you begin to focus in prayer on those in your workplace.

Come to an agreement. After your group has been meeting regularly for a period of time, you should come to an agreement on focusing your prayer in the area of evangelism. Why is this important? There are three reasons. First, this Christian prayer group that has been behind the scenes praying for others in the workplace (I call them undercover prayer agents) is now about to come out of hiding. Many in your company does not know you are meeting or have such a group…but that is all about to change. You must be aware of the changes that are coming and all agree to them. Secondly, this group will be the "prayer support" for the new evangelistic prayer group. You must agree that the ultimate goal of this Christian Prayer Group is to bring the Kingdom of God to your workplace. The individual needs of the group will be replaced with the needs of those who do not know Christ. You all need to agree on the ultimate vision of both prayer groups that meet in your workplace. And thirdly, as your coworkers come to Christ, these new converts will eventually be added to your prayer group. They will now join you in prayer for others at work who have not accepted Christ yet. The Christian Workplace Prayer Group will need to agree and be aware that the dynamics of the group is about to change. As God moves within your workplace (through your prayers), your small group is about to get a lot larger.

Approach your boss. Until now, you have not needed permission, from any higher authority in your company, to meet. You might have been gathering informally in your break room or during your lunch hour. However, if you are going to start inviting your coworkers to a planned meeting during the workday, you will need to have your boss's permission. Why is this important? First, your boss will need to give you a room to meet in (probably during your lunch hour) and secondly, it will give him or her a chance to learn more about what you are doing in these meetings. As you meet with your boss, you may indirectly inquire about things that you can pray for (the company or other personal needs he or she may have). In any regards, you need to approach your boss and let him or her know what you are planning. It is better to tell your boss now, for if your boss discovers from someone else that you are meeting, the reaction to you and your group might not be favorable.

Let me say one more thing in regards to your meeting with your boss. He or she will ask you what the purpose of your prayer group is. You and I know that the ultimate objective of this group is to bring your coworkers to Christ. However, tell your boss that the purpose of this prayer group is so others in the company can voluntarily come and have someone pray with them if they have a need. Also, let your boss know that the group will be praying that God blesses the company and him as the leader of the company. If you approach your boss with the wisdom of God (putting on your mantle of favor), he or she will most likely gladly grant you whatever you need to conduct your workplace prayer meeting.

Prepare for your first meeting. Once you have come into agreement with your Christian Workplace Prayer Group and you have obtained permission from your boss to start a new group, there are a few things you need to do before conducting your first workplace prayer evangelism meeting:

- Spend some time as a group praying that God will bless this first meeting.

- Pass out a simple flyer (with your boss's permission) announcing your meeting (time, date, and location). Be sure to mention the purpose of this meeting—to pray for anyone who may have a need. This is not a religious event, but a prayer event. In the corporate world prayer is accepted by all faiths and religions. So, stress that you are meeting to pray, not to hear a sermon.

- Prepare the meeting room. Having some light snacks is always a good way to attract people to meetings and a good icebreaker once they arrive.

Position chairs theater style—in rows, all facing forward. This arrangement helps people feel more comfortable.

Conducting your Prayer Evangelism Group meeting. Well, here is where it all gets exciting! Once your attendees have eaten, filled out their prayer request slips, and found seats, permit attendees to share what God is doing in their lives (answered prayer). This is not a time to share problems with the group, but to tell how God has improved personal situations. When the information of answered prayer starts circulating around the office, others' interest will be piqued to possibly attend the next praying meeting. This testimony period is where we can see what God is doing through our prayers.

Not only are the attendees looking forward to the "testimony time" (building their faith level), but the Christian prayer intercessors praying behind the scene are encouraged as well. Allowing time for your attendees to share their answered prayers is probably one of the most important aspects of your workplace prayer meeting's success. Be a good facilitator and keep the group on track. After the personal testimony time is over, once again collect the prayer requests and pray like you did in your first meeting. As your attendees leave, once again hand them flyers with the information about the next prayer meeting.

Sharing Christ with your attendees. You might ask, "If this is a prayer evangelism group, when does someone get the opportunity to hear about Christ and become a Christian?" You may say, "All you have talked about is prayer and sharing personal testimonies of answered prayer." Well, God is capturing the hearts of people by first meeting them right were they are (by answering their felt need prayer). After this has happened, you can simply ask if an individual would like to know more about Christ. If the response is favorable, then you can share the gospel. However, in the group setting we are describing here (remember we are not there to preach, but to pray), we handle "sharing Christ" in a different way.

In the Prayer Evangelism Group meetings that we have conducted, we have usually seen people take the next step (of knowing Christ personally) in one of two ways. Either the attendees will pick up an information card (usually placed on the snack table) that will have a box for them to check requesting a personal contact to receive more information about "having peace with God." We have found this method to be very effective. However, the most effective method has been by instructing our prayer team to just "hang out" after the meeting has ended. We have discovered that those who are seekers of God seem to "hang out" after the meeting just to talk. One thing leads to another…and the next thing you know, people are coming to Christ. We have trained our prayer team members not to leave after the meetings, but to stay and minister to those who need additional help. A prayer meeting lasts 20 to 30 minutes for our attendees, but unofficially for our prayer teams, a workplace prayer evangelism meeting usually lasts for one hour. The action takes place *after* the prayer meeting. God is so good!

The 9-5 Window

For many years, the Church has been praying for the 10/40 Window—the area of the world in which a majority of the countries have never heard the gospel of Jesus Christ. A tremendous challenge remains for the Church to continue prayer efforts in this area.

However, there is another window with an even greater potential—the Workday Window. This is the window of the marketplace. You live and breathe in the marketplace every day. The Church is getting ready to see one of the greatest harvests of souls coming from the Workday Window in the marketplace. It is time to pray like you have never prayed before. It is time to live with a sense of expectancy that God is going to use you through marketplace prayer evangelism to bring in God's end-time harvest of souls from the workplace. By the power of praying together with your coworkers you will be "getting the edge at work." Next we will look at the power of the workplace testimony!

Endnotes

1. Steve Sampson, *You Can Hear the Voice of God* (Kent, England: Sovereign World Publications, 1993), 44-54.

2. Dr. Marcus Hester, *Confronting the King of the North* (Chicago, Illinois: Hester International Publications, 1999), 35.

3. Bill Hybels, *Becoming a Contagious Christian* (Grand Rapids, Michigan: Zondervan Publishing House, 1994), 97.

4. Ed Silvoso, *Prayer Evangelism* (Ventura, California: Regal Books, 2000), 52.

Chapter 13

THE POWER OF THE WORKPLACE TESTIMONY

For He established a testimony in Jacob, and appointed a law in Israel, which He commanded our fathers, that they should make them known to their children (Psalm 78:5).

As I was growing up in the Baptist church, every Wednesday night we had testimony time. Testimony time involved the members of the church standing up one at a time to give a praise report of what God was doing in our lives. The purpose of the testimony was not to brag on ourselves, but to brag on God and about the great things He was doing. Others in the room who heard the testimonies were encouraged and edified. The word *testimony* means "something given or done to show gratitude (appreciation) or a statement made to establish a fact (declaration)."[1] God established a testimony in the life of Jacob, the great Jewish patriarch, but I have some good news. God is establishing a fresh and compelling testimony in your life as a marketplace leader, and the Church needs to hear about it.

In this next Marketplace movement, God will restore the power of the personal testimony. When church leaders get a revelation of this word, then the Marketplace movement will be propelled into its next level. Let me give you some blessings and benefits of the personal marketplace testimony:

1. *It releases faith to other marketplace ministers.*

Let us hold fast the profession of our faith without wavering; (for He is faithful that promised) (Hebrews 10:23).

If a personal testimony is communicated in the spirit of giving glory to God, then something is released in the atmosphere that encourages others as well. The persuasive influence is something like this: "If it can happen to them, maybe it can happen to me." Others will feel encouraged to step out in their workplace to attempt great things for God as well.

Also faith is released when the person giving the personal testimony is someone to whom you can relate. I asked an advertising company why so many of the actors on their TV ads were not necessarily gorgeous people. Many of the actors and actresses were overweight and others were bald. The advertising director said, "People buy from people who are like themselves. Most people are not like Hollywood stars, but rather a little overweight and missing some hair on top." It's the same way in the Church. People can respond to others who are like themselves. In this next Marketplace movement, not only will we hear testimony from our marketplace ministers on a regular basis, but also those giving the testimony will be like you and me (everyday saints trying to serve the Lord in their workplaces).

The Church has been *advertising* the "super saint" in front of their congregations in order to draw the crowds, but this is about to stop. It is time we hear from the "everyday" saints and listen carefully to what they have to say. These are the ones who are on the front lines of God's advance into the world; what they have to say has tremendous value. Pastors, if you will allow for marketplace testimonies in your meetings, this single action will help your congregation be impacted by the newly emerging Marketplace movement. It will ignite a spirit of faith in your congregation, encouraging others to step out in their own work environments. Yes, it is important to preach the concept, but it so much more powerful to hear testimonies from those who are experiencing the presence of God in the workplace. Faith is then released to help others be all they can be in the workplace.

2. *It motivates other marketplace ministers.*

But charge Joshua, and encourage him, and strengthen him: for he shall go over before this people, and he shall cause them to inherit the land which thou shalt see (Deuteronomy 3:28).

Not only will the personal marketplace testimony release faith, it will motivate other marketplace ministers as well. It may be the very answer that someone else is seeking in order to solve his own problem. As a preacher and businessman, after I conclude my meetings, people tell me that something I said in my testimony was the answer to their problem. I had no idea how I had helped this individual (but God did). God allowed me to say something in my testimony that encouraged and motivated this individual. The personal marketplace testimony will encourage and motivate other marketplace ministers.

3. *It takes the marketplace minister out of "hiding."*

And I will give thee the treasures of darkness, and hidden riches of secret places, that thou mayest know that I, the Lord, which call thee by thy name, am the God of Israel (Isaiah 45:3).

Next you will see that church leadership will begin to hear your thoughts, ideas, and dreams for the marketplace, and other marketplace leaders will be inspired by who you are and what you desire. First, let me address the idea of church leadership hearing you. As a pastor for many years, I would speak sometimes two or three times a week. Just a little side note here: Preachers have a tendency to speak a lot, but rarely do we take time to listen to those to whom we preach. There is such power in the listening ear. The more pastors allow the marketplace ministers the opportunity to speak and the more they hear their hearts, the more they will become in tune with what God is doing in their congregations. This knowledge will empower pastors in their own ministry to the people, and it will certainly communicate more effectively how much they care for the congregation. To be effective spiritual leaders, we must stop speaking so much and start listening a lot more. In our meetings, it is essential that we allow time to hear our marketplace ministers. If we don't, we are simply sending a message to them that what they have to say and contribute is not important. This issue has weighed heavy on my heart, so heavy that I will be releasing a new book entitled *Why Men Don't Come to Church*. This new book will address how to attract men back to our churches. Often we do not make businessmen feel important. We don't listen to them. These are men who are active all week long. They are used to being involved and listened to. If we do not make room for their gifts and if we do not hear their hearts, then why should they come to our churches? Rather, it is love and a listening ear that will attract them.

When I was working in the medical field at Dupont, I had an experience that changed my life. For many years I had been selling medical equipment to doctors. I traveled all over this country and was a good salesman. However, one day the company asked if I would like to be a sales manager. Realizing the pay increase, I gladly accepted this new position. However, little did I realize that my life was about to change. I thought I was a good salesman, but after becoming a sales manager, I discovered that I was lacking in many areas. As a sales manager, my job was not to sell anymore, but watch and manage others as they sold. Most of the day, my time would consist of going along on sales calls to observe my salesmen making their presentations. Afterward, the salesman and I would discuss how he had done. Becoming a sales manager allowed me to discover the "gift of listening." By observing and watching others all day, I noticed how much we talk, but do not listen. Many of us, including me, are more interested in what we have to say than what *others* have to say. That experience left an indelible impression on my life. I learned the power of listening. If you want to be a good leader, whether in church or business, you must make way for others to speak more and you must listen more. You might just be surprised how much you will learn.

Secondly, as marketplace ministers speak more publicly, not only will the leadership of the church begin to know and hear their heart, but also other marketplace ministers will discover the "hidden treasure" within them. Many times after one of my meetings, I will go visit in the foyer to discover businessmen and women meeting one anther for the very first time. Some of these people have been members of the same church for years. I will hear them saying something like, "I did not know you were from Texas. I grew up there, too." Or I will hear, "How long have you been in the banking industry? Do you know that my dad was a banker and I am, too?"

I call these encounters *networking God's way*! Marketplace leaders are listening to other marketplace leaders (not necessarily with their ears...but with their hearts). Let me reiterate, when we make room for marketplace leaders to give their testimony in our churches, something happens: Faith is released, others are encouraged, and the "hidden treasures" in others are revealed.

How to Share Your Marketplace Testimony

As a preacher's kid growing up in North Carolina, I remember my Sunday school teacher giving me an assignment to write out my personal testimony of how I became a Christian. She gave me some instructions on how to write it and how long it should be. Before I give you a list of some *do's* and *don'ts* of giving your marketplace testimony, let me make one statement. This testimony should be about how God is using you in the marketplace, either in your kingly or priestly role, not about how you got saved. A marketplace testimony is for the purpose of proclaiming to others how God is working through you in the marketplace. With that in mind, here are a few helpful hints:

- Don't be afraid. Standing before people can be a horrifying experience and can paralyze you before you even get up to speak. However, if we are going to start proclaiming to others what God is doing through our lives in the workplace, we are going to have to get over our fears. One simple way to do this is to first practice your message with a friend. Then let that person give you suggestions for improving your communication. The public testimony in the safe environment of your church can be the first step in overcoming your fear of speaking in public.

- Be aware of your time. Make sure that you ask the leader how long you should speak. One of businesspeople's most valuable possessions is their time. Time is money and money is time. Be respectful to your leader and those in your audience by respecting the time limit given to you. Trust me, if you abuse your time limit, you may not be asked to speak again—no matter how good your testimony is.

- Ask yourself, "Who is my audience?" Your audience will determine the makeup of your speech. Your audience may be all Christians or all un-churched folk. Your message might not change, but your delivery will be based on who is in your audience.

- What is the purpose of your testimony? One of the classic mistakes that speakers make is spending more time on the problem than on the solution. Ask yourself, "How will my talk help someone else?" Would I listen to someone else give my speech? Keep to the point and keep on the subject. A good personal testimony will grab someone's heart, as you reveal how "God and you" made it through the "fire" together.

- Don't take yourself too seriously. Zig Ziglar, one of the greatest speakers in the world (making over $50,000 per speech) once said, "If I cannot get my audience laughing within the first 30 seconds of my speech, then I failed that day as a speech maker."[2] When people laugh (not laughing *at* you, but *with* you), something is triggered in the human physique that allows us to "swallow the medicine" a little bit easier. Why do you think pharmaceutical companies mix grape and cherry flavoring into our children's medicine? Well, it makes the medicine a little easier to take. This is a good lesson for speakers. Be sure you are mixing in a little sweetness with your words. The sweetness of the audience's laughter can relax us. Do not take yourself too seriously. People will be more open to receive you and your message if they can touch the human side of you.

- Challenge your audience. I remember telling one of my salesmen after a sales call, "You made a great presentation and the doctor loved your product, but you never asked for the order. You never got a commitment from the doctor." Many times when we give our personal testimonies and the audience loves what we had to say, giving them action steps to follow, we fail to finish our speech and close the sale, by not asking for a commitment from the audience. Good speakers challenge their audiences in some capacity and elicit some kind of personal response.

Getting Your Personal Testimony Back at Work

Ye are the salt of the earth: but if the salt have lost his savour, wherewith shall it be salted? it is thenceforth good for nothing, but to be cast out, and to be trodden under foot of men. Ye are the light of the world. A city that is set on an hill cannot be hid. Neither do men light a candle, and put it under a bushel, but on a candlestick; and it giveth light unto all that are in the house. Let your light so shine before men, that they may see your good works, and glorify your Father which is in heaven (Matthew 5:13-16).

How do you get something back that you have lost? First of all, you must realize that you lost it (your testimony for God). I would like to deal with how to retrieve and restore a bad testimony. Some of us might have lost our testimony by either joining in with others at work on a "bad joke," gossip, lying, anger, or stealing something from our employer. I am sure that we all have done something at work that we wished we could take back. When we know in our hearts that we have not acted in a Christ-like manner at work, the tendency is to hide our faith from that point on. We feel guilty and ashamed. We feel that everyone knows our faults and is judging us. We have lost our boldness for Christ.

And now, Lord, behold their threatenings: and grant unto Thy servants, that with all boldness they may speak Thy word (Acts 4:29).

If we are going to be effective for God at work, we have to walk in boldness under God's authority. We have to be willing to restore our personal testimony in the workplace so that once again we can be "salt and light." Here are a few steps to help you get your personal testimony back at work:

- First acknowledge that you have weakened and lost your testimony. Many businesspeople are so used to being ineffective for Christ that they do not even realize they have lost their personal testimony at work. Sunday they may act one way, but on Monday they act like everyone else. To distinguish you from your non-Christian coworker would be impossible. If this is you, then you need to do a self-examination of how you have been "salt and light" in your workplace. Be honest with yourself about the state of your personal testimony at work. Declare to the Lord that you have missed the mark. Cry out to the Lord, "Help me get my testimony back at work!"

- Let the Holy Spirit reveal to you how and when you lost your testimony. In your quiet time in the morning with God, let the Holy Spirit reveal to you situations at work that have caused you to lose your testimony. Once again, it might be something that everyone at work knows about (or maybe only one individual knows), or it might be something you have done in secret. Whatever it may be, acknowledge your sins to the Lord. Simply agree with God that His standard of holiness at work is higher than yours.

- Confess your sins to the Lord and ask for forgiveness. "If we confess our sins, He is faithful and just to forgive us our sins, and to cleanse us from all unrighteousness" (1 John 1:9).

- Once you acknowledge your sins (as the Holy Spirit has revealed them to you), you must then make it right with God. How do you do that? Simply by confessing your sins and asking God to forgive you. God has already made provision for your sins on the cross. All we have to do is confess them and then leave them (at the foot of the cross). Once you do this, you will experience an immediate peace with God. You will literally feel His grace upon your life once again. New boldness and power will come flooding back into your life. In your heart, you will know that your relationship with God is right again.

- Confess your sins to your coworkers. You have already acknowledged that you have lost your testimony. You have allowed the Holy Spirit to reveal to you where you have missed it. You have confessed your sins to God. However, if your sin involves someone else (individual or group), you need to make it right with them as well. "Confess your faults one to another [your coworkers], and pray one for another [your coworkers], that ye may be healed. The effectual fervent prayer of a righteous man availeth much" (James 5:16). You have to use wisdom in how to do this. For example, if you got angry with someone at work, then you need to go to that person privately and ask him or her to forgive you. If you were angry in a group, as the group meets again, you need to ask the whole group to forgive you. Just making it right with God will not get your testimony back at work. If your sin involves someone else, you need to go to the next step and make it right with the person (or persons) as well.

- Confess that you are going to maintain a strong and convincing personal testimony at work and start walking in your dual calling as a king and priest in your workplace. Yes, you may "blow it" again. That is okay. Just follow these steps again and immediately recapture your personal testimony at work. Remember, you cannot be a marketplace minister for others until you first become a marketplace minister yourself. You cannot lead your co-workers to the Lord until first your own relationship with the Lord is right.

Pastor...It Is Okay to Let Them Loose!

We have discussed in this chapter that the marketplace testimony will be one of the key ingredients that will help propel the Marketplace movement into its next level. We have discussed that a good marketplace testimony will release faith to your audience, motivate others, and reveal the "hidden treasures" in you. We have discussed some of the steps that you might take as you prepare to give your marketplace testimony. And we have discussed how to recapture your personal testimony at work so you can be a light in a dark place once again.

However, why are we not seeing more marketplace testimonies in the church today if this is so important to the movement? Well, there are several reasons, but one main reason lies at the feet of the senior pastor of the church. Remember, as senior pastor of Family Life International for many years, I have the right to talk to other senior pastors. Many times church leaders are afraid of what people will say when they are released to speak from the pulpit—not that they will say something harmful about the pastor or the church, but that either they speak too long or their speech misses the mark. For whatever reason, if we are going to see regular marketplace testimonies coming from our meetings, then the senior leaders of the church are going to have to run the risk and make room in the meetings for marketplace testimony. *Either loose your congregation or you will lose your congregation!* Pastor, if a bird is ever going to fly, then you have to give him room to exercise his wings. He may fall on his face, but you still have to give the bird the opportunity. Remember that someone once made room for you—now is the time to return the favor. Likewise, pastors, if you are going to have any success in this matter of the marketplace testimony, you will have to give the marketplace ministers in your church an opportunity to let others know what God is doing in their environment. At Marketplace Movement Network we are working on a curriculum that we will be implementing into churches shortly. It will give our marketplace ministers a safe haven to practice sharing their marketplace testimonies in front of others.

Are you ready to start proclaiming what God is doing in the marketplace? Pastors, are you going to set your marketplace leaders free to share their testimonies? *It is time to hear from our marketplace ministers, and we must make room in our meetings to hear them!*

Is your expectancy level increasing? Are you starting to get a sense of what God is up to in the modern-day Marketplace movement? Marketplace prayer is increasing all over the world. Marketplace testimony is starting to be heard again in meetings all over the country. God is getting His Church prepared, raising up both marketplace kings and priests for one of the greatest harvest of souls from the marketplace the Church has ever seen. *God is saving the best for last!*

Endnotes

1. Victoria Neufeldt, *Webster's New World Dictionary* (Cleveland, Ohio: Warner Books, 1990), 610.

2. Zig Ziglar, *See You at the Top* (Gretna, Louisiana: Pelican Publishing, 1995), 76.

Chapter 14

THE BEST IS YET AHEAD

My little children, of whom I travail in birth again until Christ be formed in you (Galatians 4:19).

As the Body of Christ is moving into this modern-day Marketplace movement, my spirit is so excited! I love to see God doing something new within the Body of Christ. There truly is such a spirit of expectancy in the air. God is so looking forward to this next move in His Church—the Marketplace movement. He is looking for some modern-day marketplace kings and priests to start putting the God factor to work in the marketplace. Once that happens we will see how God will start showing up with "wonders and miracles." *God wants you to get the edge!* You are one of His children! He desires to show Himself big through you at your place of work. He is truly saving the best for last! The Church is about to see one of the greatest wealth transfers back into the Church that she has ever seen. The Church will experience one of the greatest additions of souls that it has ever witnessed. Yes, the best is yet ahead!

My wife's labor with our third child, Jacob, was a little longer than expected. I remember walking the floors of the hospital waiting for my son to be born. The spirit of expectancy was raging high within me. The wait was excruciating. Finally, the doctor called me into the delivery room to help my wife with that final push needed to bring my son into this world. Even though Jacob's birth had taken longer than expected, he was well worth the wait.

In similar fashion, God is waiting with expectancy for His end-time revival to come forth from the marketplace. Like an expectant father, He is waiting for the "birth" of all His new children who will enter the Kingdom of God from the marketplace.

Saving the Best Wine for Last

Everyone brings out the choice wine first and then the cheaper wine after the guests have had too much to drink; but you have saved the best till now (John 2:10 NIV).

Jesus' first miracle was turning the water into wine. Many Christians have misunderstood this first miracle. As so often happens the Church gets involved in focusing in on the secondary issues rather than the primary. We hotly debate all the different facets of this event and miss the miracle and true reason for the event. One of the interesting things about this first miracle was the *quality* of wine that Jesus created from the water. Not only did Jesus create wine from water, He created a *premium* wine as well. In the Jewish celebrations in those days it was customary for the host of the party to bring out the best wines for his guests. As the party went into the night and the host needed more wine, he served the guests from the cheap stock found in the basement. Jesus surprised this host by not only turning the water into wine, but by creating the best wine (premium wine) for the guests who still remained at the party. Jesus saved the best wine for last! Likewise, the Body of Christ in the last five hundred years has experienced some exciting movements—the Prophetic movement and the Apostolic movement, to name a few—but with the Marketplace movement, God has saved one of the best outpourings of His Spirit for our generation.

Hope Deferred

Hope deferred maketh the heart sick: but when the desire cometh, it is a tree of life (Proverbs 13:12).

Have you ever had a promise from God that you keep expecting to be fulfilled, but nothing ever happens? Have you had a desire that you felt God put in your heart that never materialized? Did you once have faith to see the plan of God for your life manifested, but now that faith seems dry and distant? Did you have great expectations for God moving on your behalf, but are still waiting?[1] God calls this feeling that you may be experiencing *hope deferred*. And this feeling of self-pity can literally make you spiritually, emotionally, and physically sick.

However, if you are feeling hopeless, God is about to change all that. I have two exciting words for you: *but God!*

My flesh and my heart faileth: but God is the strength of my heart, and my portion for ever (Psalm 73:26).

For indeed he was sick nigh unto death: but God had mercy on him; and not on him only, but on me also, lest I should have sorrow upon sorrow (Philippians 2:27).

But as for you, ye thought evil against me; but God meant it unto good, to bring to pass, as it is this day, to save much people alive (Genesis 50:20).

One of the most faith-building phrases in the Bible is "but God...." It is in these amazing words that we find hope for what lies ahead. Whatever your circumstances at work may be like, or whatever your circumstances at school may look like, or whatever your circumstances in your neighborhood may seem like, I have some good news to share with you. "But God" is about to show up big in your life! "But God" is about to show up in your workplace. "But God" is about to show up at your school. "But God" is about to show up once again in your neighborhood. Keep your eyes on God and what He has in store for you. He wants to bless you. He wants you to take part in His end-time plan in the marketplace and then this will be a "tree of life" for you.

Releasing Supernatural Power

And with great power gave the apostles witness of the resurrection of the Lord Jesus: and great grace was upon them all (Acts 4:33).

As the Church is going through a transition process, many Christians are waiting on God to show up in their businesses, marriages, schools, and neighborhoods.

Many are waiting on God, but remember God is waiting on you. As soon as the Church gets hold of this new revelation of the Marketplace movement and starts ministering outside of the four walls of the church, then watch out! Have you ever heard of "open heavens"? That is what is about to occur over the Body of Christ if we get hold of this marketplace message. A great rip is going to occur in the heavenly skies and God is about to pour out His blessings through that newly created "open heaven." I can almost see the finger of the Father piercing through the veil between Heaven and earth as He prepares to unleash His power on His people.

As a pastor, I remember praying for the sick or someone in need during the altar call at the end of the service. And this is good. As Christians, we are supposed to call on the "elders of the church" to pray for us when we are sick (see Jas. 5:14). However, when God's Church starts taking His power into the workplace, the schools, the political arenas, our neighborhoods, and sports centers, I believe God will pour out His great grace and great power onto His Body like nothing we have ever seen before. Are you waiting on God? Just maybe, God is waiting on you to take His message to the marketplace.

Your Dual Calling

And hath made us kings [marketplace managers] *and priests* [marketplace ministers] *unto God and His Father; to Him be glory and dominion for ever and ever. Amen* (Revelation 1:6).

One of my main reasons for writing this book is so that you, the marketplace Christian, will be able to catch hold of the revelation that you have two callings on your life:

—*to bring in wealth for the Kingdom of God (as a king).*

—*to be a minister in the workplace (as a priest).*

When you realize that you have two callings on your life, it is then important that you begin to walk in both of your callings as well. With the Marketplace movement, God is pouring out His great grace and great power for you to be all you can be in Christ.

As you walk in your dual callings in the marketplace, excitement is building in Heaven! Some of you are starting to catch hold of this new revelation and are getting excited about what God is about to do through you in the marketplace. But I know a group who is even more excited than you are—that is the host of angels in Heaven who are celebrating the day of the great harvest.

> *Wherefore seeing we also are compassed about with so great a cloud of witnesses* [heavenly host of angels], *let us lay aside every weight, and the sin which doth so easily beset us, and let us run with patience the race that is set before us* (Hebrews 12:1).

Just as the Church is being prepared for the next great harvest of souls coming from the marketplace, Heaven is getting prepared as well. Excitement is running high in Heaven! When I played football in college, it was always exciting for me to be on the field on a Saturday afternoon and look out in the stands to see all our fans cheering for us. The cheerleaders would be cheering hard and the band would be playing something exhilarating to cheer on our team. Several times a year, our team would have to go away to play our games at the stadiums of the opposing school. Those games were always harder to win because our cheering section (our fans) was not around. Yes, a few of our fans would travel to those away games, but of course, our fan base was drastically dwindled.

Does a cheering section matter to your performance? You bet is does! You will notice in pro football that all the teams will literally fight to win home field advantage. Well, as the Church enters its "play-off" season, God has made sure that the Church has home field advantage. God has positioned his host of angels in position to cheer you on as you play in the game of your life—the marketplace bowl. Are you excited yet? I know a group (God's heavenly host) who is there cheering you on to win in the game of life. The angels are already rejoicing (cheering you on) in excitement over what they are about to witness, as the Church enters the marketplace (the marketplace bowl).

Jesus Is Waiting on You

And this gospel of the kingdom shall be preached in all the world for a witness unto all nations; and then shall the end come (Matthew 24:14).

Many church leaders agree that Jesus will return to this earth. However, many church leaders do not agree *when* He will return or how He will return. However, I do know one thing, the Bible clearly states that Jesus *will not* return until the gospel is preached to the entire world and that includes the marketplaces of the world. As Christians, it is not time to start thinking of going to Heaven or about Jesus' return. It is time for His Body to focus on the work that lies ahead in the marketplace. Yes, I want to go to Heaven one day and be with Jesus (just like anybody else), but I don't want to go until I have finished my work here on earth (reaching as many marketplace leaders as I can). Are you waiting on God? God is waiting on you (His Church) to finish the work of the Great Commission.

And Jesus came and spake unto them, saying, All power is given unto Me in heaven and in earth. Go ye therefore, and teach all nations, baptizing them in the name of the Father, and of the Son, and of the Holy Ghost: teaching them to observe all things whatsoever I have commanded you: and, lo, I am with you always, even unto the end of the world. Amen (Matthew 28:18-20).

Jesus cannot come again until every nation hears the gospel. With the Marketplace movement, the Body of Christ is moving now one step closer to seeing the fulfillment of Matthew 24:14. We are expanding into new territory as we seek to expose our coworkers to the Gospel of the Kingdom. The Church's level of expectancy is rising. Jesus' level of expectation is rising as well. With this next Marketplace movement, Jesus is seeing Himself one step closer to being with His Church (the Bride of Christ). Do you long to be with Jesus? Do you think Jesus longs to be with His Church? Well, let us all get to work and finish the job of the Great Commission (as we pull in the net of souls from the marketplace).

City Transformation

As the Church walks into this frontier of the marketplace, our entire culture has the possibility of being transformed. The Church must move from *church* transformation to *city* transformation. Until every fiber of our city is touched by the power of God, then we have not reached the full magnitude of the Marketplace movement. Not only is God recruiting the whole Church to do His work, but God is also moving His saints from the confines of the church and positioning them in the streets of the marketplace.

In *The God Factor...Getting the Edge at Work*, I have attempted to take you one step closer to seeing God's mandate for His Church being completed—the Great Commission!

In this new Marketplace movement, God is recruiting the whole Body of Christ to take the whole city for Christ. In the advance into the marketplace, no one will be a bench warmer. Everyone will be involved in this next move of God. Not only will everyone be involved, but God also is moving His influence from the boundaries of the church to now extend His influence into your city—the marketplace. God will not limit His power and influence to just the local church; He wants to influence every fiber of our lives, communities, and cities. God is a big God and is *about to break out of His box (the four walls of our churches).*

Jesus' second coming is closer than we think. God is ready to come back again to a powerful and victorious Church. God is ready to finish the job of the Great Commission. God is calling you to be a part of His end-time army of marketplace managers (wealth builders) and marketplace ministers (soul winners). Are you willing to take a step of faith and be used by God in your workplace, school, or neighborhood? Are you willing to take your position in one of the greatest events that the Church has ever seen—the Marketplace movement!?

The God Factor (getting the edge at work) is about to change your 9-5 life...forever!

Your Next Step

What is your next step? If you feel a sense of urgency to walk in this new movement in the marketplace, then you are right where you need to be. However, I do not want to leave you "dangling like a fish out of water." Here are some suggestions to help you discover your dual calling in this Marketplace movement:

- Re-read this book several times, asking the Holy Spirit for direction about your role to play in God's end-time harvest of souls from the marketplace. Get this message deep into your soul and let it become a living revelation for you.

- Read other books to help you get further clarity regarding God's end-time harvest of souls. (See recommendations at the back of this book.)

- Ask your pastor how he or she is preparing for God's end-time harvest of souls from the marketplace.

- Visit other churches or ministries that are teaching on how to be *marketplace ministers* and/or *marketplace managers*.

- Attend conferences and seminars that will help you further understand this new Marketplace movement.

It is my prayer that this message will revolutionize your life and that you will never again be able to look at your job in the same old mundane way. Let these words sink deep into your spirit as you learn to "get the edge at work" with *the God Factor.*

Endnote

1. Chuck Pierce and Rebecca Sytsema, *The Best Is Yet Ahead* (Colorado Springs, Colorado: Wagner Publications, 2001), 61.

TRENDS THAT WILL EMERGE WITH THE FULL MANIFESTATION OF THE MARKETPLACE MOVEMENT

It is imperative that marketplace leaders come into their appointed positions of leadership in the church as well as in their cities. In order to do this, they must be identified and released. When marketplace leaders come into their places, the city will experience great blessing. Individuals must begin to walk in these callings with confidence and boldness.

The *marketplace manager* and the *marketplace minister* must be confirmed and strengthened. The church will advance and experience great breakthroughs as a result of these marketplace leaders coming forth. The saints will experience a new level of perfecting, maturity, and release and thus be one step closer to fulfilling the Great Commission. We must align ourselves with these marketplace leaders and the Marketplace movement.

I see the following 14 trends emerging in the Church with the full restoration of the marketplace minister (kings and priests):

- Greater experience of wonders and miracles as the Church begins ministering outside the four walls of its buildings. People will especially witness increased miracles in the workplace, school, and political settings.

- Release of great grace to handle finances for the Kingdom of God as huge amounts of wealth for the advance of the Kingdom are transferred to the Church. The Joseph/Daniel Company will arise to fund God's end-time harvest of souls.

- The everyday saints will assume their positions as *marketplace managers* and *marketplace ministers* (dual callings). The one-man ministry will cease to exist. The term *full-time* minister will refer to the entire Body of Christ rather than a selected few. Body ministry will become a normal phenomenon of the Church.

- Financial Distribution Centers that train the Body to handle finances for the Kingdom of God will become mainstream in most evangelical churches. Cities will turn back to the Church for financial help as the many social and political needs increase.

- New positions in the Church will emerge—ministers of finance and marketplace ministers. Marketplace apostles will be recognized in the Body of Christ just as modern-day evangelists, teachers, pastors, prophets and territorial apostles are today. As the Church recognizes that it is in the Second Apostolic Age, God's new government will form in the nuclear church as well as the extended church.

- Kingdom Wisdom Centers will become mainstream in most evangelical churches, too. Training centers to equip the marketplace leaders to minister to God's end-time harvest of souls will spring up in most churches around the world.

- Fivefold ministers will assume their roles as trainers and equippers rather than just deliverers of "felt need" messages. Leaders will begin assuming their true callings as trainers to the Body of Christ. As marketplace leaders realize their dual callings (marketplace managers and marketplace ministers), the Church will experience a leadership shift that will shake every fabric of the modern-day Church.

- Separation of the Church and marketplace will fade away. God and the things of God will be accepted back into schools, workplaces and political arenas.

- The terms *clergy* and *laity* will disappear as the saints assume equal roles in the Body of Christ rather than one position being superior over the other.

There will still be an order of spiritual authority, but the attitude that one person is better than another will cease to exist.

- Christians will assume new roles of leadership in the political, social, business and military realms. *The God factor will be socially accepted as a legitimate tool for solving problems in society and the workplace.*

- City Transformation will occur. Whole cites will experience revival and turn toward God. Miracles that occurred in the Book of Acts will become "common place" in our cities once again.

- The fear of the Lord will become real in many lives. Great persecutions will increase upon the Christian, but at the same time, more people will become Christians than at any time in history.

- Prayer intercessors will emerge in the marketplace. The need for prayer covering and strategic prayer plans for businesses will become just as normal as prayer for churches and their leaders are today. Marketplace intercessors will not only cover businesses, but will also train others to pray for the release of the wealth and souls in the marketplace.

- Personal testimonies from the Body of Christ will be a major ingredient that will perpetuate the marketplace movement. Accounts of how God is working in people's lives will release great faith to the rest of the Church to help others fulfill their dual calling in this marketplace movement.

RECOMMENDED READING LIST

Anointed for Business, Ed Silvoso (Regal)

Apostles of the City, Peter Wagner (Wagner Publications)

Becoming a Contagious Christian, Bill Hybels (Zondervan)

The Best Is Yet Ahead, Chuck Pierce (Wagner Publications)

The Day of the Saints, Dr. Bill Hamon (Destiny Image)

Effective Fervent Prayer, Mary Alice Isleib (Isleib Publishing)

End Time Warriors, John Kelly (Renew)

Future War of the Church, Chuck Pierce (Renew)

The Gatekeepers, Nate Wolf (Insight Publishing)

God@Work, Rich Marshall (Destiny Image)

The God Chasers, Tommy Tenney (Destiny Image)

The God Factor, Dr. Marcus Hester (Destiny Image)

God's Provocative Plan for Wealth, Ann Bandini (C.E.O. Publishing)

Marketplace Ministers, Paul Gazelka (Creation House)

Moving in the Apostolic, John Eckhardt (Renew)

Plucking the Eagle's Wings, Perry Stone (Voice of Evangelism)

Possessing the Gates of the Enemy, Cindy Jacobs (Chosen Books)

Prayer Evangelism, Ed Silvoso (Regal)

Primary Purpose, Ted Haggard (Creation House)

The Purpose Driven Church, Rick Warren (Zondervan)

Religious Freedom in the Workplace, Jay Sekulow (American Center for Law and Justice)

Spheres of Authority, Peter Wagner (Wagner Publications)

Supporting Christians at Work, Mark Greene (London Institute)

That None Should Perish, Ed Silvoso (Regal)

Today God Is First, Os Hillman (Destiny Image)

Worship Warrior, Chuck Pierce (Regal)

OTHER BOOKS BY DR. MARCUS HESTER...

Confronting the King of the North (Hester Publishing)

Crossing the Goal Line (Hester Publishing)

How to Finish the Job (Hester Publishing)

Books Coming Soon by Dr. Marcus Hester...

Balancing It All...Making Life Work

Beyond the Blessing

Catching the Whales

Discerning Robbers and Thieves

The God Factor II...Keeping the Edge at Work

Why Men Don't Go to Church

Dr. Marcus Hester is the president of the Marketplace Movement Network (www.MarketplaceMovement.com) and CEO of Hester International Enterprises (www.HesterIntl.com). You can receive information about products, and scheduling and training opportunities by contacting Dr. Marcus Hester:

Marketplace Movement Network
1105 Milwaukee Ave.
Riverwoods, IL 60015 (USA)

847-267-9430 Office
847-267-9432 Fax
www.MarketplaceMovement.com
Marcus@MarketplaceMovement.com

GOD@WORK

by Rich Marshall

God is showing up in places we have never imagined. We thought He was just for Sunday church or mid-week study. But God is showing up in small businesses and on construction sites, in schools and in politics. He is in factories and at checkout counters, at nurses' stations and the stock exchange. God is showing up everywhere outside of where we expect Him to be.

So what does it mean?

We serve a God who is not acting like we thought He should act.

This book is an awesome tool of discovery to learn not only what God

wants, but how we can cooperate with His plan for the nations, not just the Church.

Discover how He wants you to step into a realm of ministry and fulfillment you have never dreamed possible. Learn how your work is the powerful dynamic of God's purposes for your life.

This book is the beginning of new possibilities for those who are willing to see that God is bigger than they thought He was.

ISBN 0-7684-2101-2

TODAY, GOD IS FIRST
by Os Hillman

Yes, we all know that God is first every day, or at least He should be first. But can I be real for just a moment? Sometimes it is hard to keep Him first in my day. It is a struggle to see Him in the circumstances of my job. I need help to bring the reality if my Lord into my place of work.

Os Hillman has the uncanny ability to write to the readers circumstance, and exactly to their needs. He helps them to see from God's view. Strengthening and encouraging to both see God and invite Him into the everyday trials and struggles of work.

So take this book to work, put it on your desk or table. Every day, just before you tackle the mountains before you, pause long enough to remind yourself, Today, God Is First.

ISBN 0-7684-3006-2

Additional copies of this book and other
book titles from DESTINY IMAGE are
available at your local bookstore.

For a bookstore near you, call 1-800-722-6774

Send a request for a catalog to:

Destiny Image® Publishers, Inc.

P.O. Box 310
Shippensburg, PA 17257-0310

*"Speaking to the Purposes of God for This
Generation and for the Generations to Come"*

For a complete list of our titles,
visit us at www.destinyimage.com